Apple® One

by Dwight Spivey

for dummies®
A Wiley Brand

Apple® One For Dummies®

Published by **John Wiley & Sons, Inc.**, 111 River Street, Hoboken, NJ 07030-5774, www.wiley.com

For general information on our other products and services, please contact our Customer Care Department within the U.S. at 877-762-2974, outside the U.S. at 317-572-3993, or fax 317-572-4002. For technical support, please visit https://hub.wiley.com/community/support/dummies.

Wiley publishes in a variety of print and electronic formats and by print-on-demand. Some material included with standard print versions of this book may not be included in e-books or in print-on-demand. If this book refers to media such as a CD or DVD that is not included in the version you purchased, you may download this material at http://booksupport.wiley.com. For more information about Wiley products, visit www.wiley.com.

Library of Congress Control Number: 2021936481

ISBN: 978-1-119-80094-1; ISBN (ePDF): 978-1-119-80095-8; ISBN (ePub): 978-1-119-80096-5

Manufactured in the United States of America

SKY10026476_042621

Table of Contents

INTRODUCTION . . . 1
- About This Book . . . 2
- Foolish Assumptions . . . 3
- Icons Used in This Book . . . 4
- Beyond the Book . . . 4
- Where to Go from Here . . . 5

PART 1: SERVICES, PLEASE! . . . 7

CHAPTER 1: **Getting a Handle on Apple Services** . . . 9
- What Are Apple Services? . . . 10
- Apple Services in a Nutshell . . . 11
  - Apple Music . . . 11
  - Apple TV+ . . . 12
  - Apple Arcade . . . 13
  - Apple News+ . . . 14
  - Apple Fitness+ . . . 15
  - iCloud . . . 16
- Apple One Plans and Pricing . . . 18

CHAPTER 2: **Cool Devices for Cool Services** . . . 19
- Finding Devices Ready for Apple One . . . 19
  - iPhone . . . 20
  - iPad . . . 22
  - Mac . . . 23
  - Apple TV . . . 25
  - Apple Watch . . . 26
  - PCs . . . 28
  - Android . . . 29
- Apple One on the WWW . . . 30

PART 2: ARE YOU NOT ENTERTAINED? . . . 33

CHAPTER 3: **Get Yo Groove On** . . . 35
- Access Apple Music . . . 36
  - iPhone and iPad . . . 36
  - Mac . . . 37

Windows 37
Android 38
Website 39
Groovin' with Your Tunes 39
iPhone, iPad, and Android 40
Mac, Windows, and Website 43

CHAPTER 4: **Not Just TV — TV+!** 45
Access Apple TV+ 46
iPhone and iPad 46
Mac 47
Apple TV 47
Smart TVs and gaming consoles 48
Non-Apple streaming devices 49
Website 49
Watching Your Apple Gogglebox 50
iPhone and iPad 50
Mac 51
Other devices and platforms 52

CHAPTER 5: **Get Your Head in the Game!** 53
Access Apple Arcade 54
iPhone and iPad 54
Mac 55
Apple TV 55
Finding and Downloading Games 57
iPhone and iPad 57
Mac 58
Apple TV 59

PART 3: LIFESTYLES OF THE FIT AND INFORMED 61

CHAPTER 6: **Staying Informed with Apple News+** 63
Access News and News+ 64
iPhone and iPad 64
Mac 65
All the News That's Fit to Print (or View) 66
Perusing the magazine rack 66

CHAPTER 7: **Fitness Fanatics +** 73
Access Fitness+ 74
Supported devices 74
iPhone and iPad 74

Apple TV 75
Finding and Starting Workouts 75
Finding a workout 76
Starting and tracking a workout 78

PART 4: EVERY ICLOUD HAS A SILVER LINING 81

CHAPTER 8: **Walking on iCloud Nine** 83
What Is iCloud? 84
The Storage Conundrum 86
Signing In and Accessing iCloud 87
Signing in to iCloud 87
Accessing iCloud 90

CHAPTER 9: **Buckle Up and Drive!** 93
Accessing iCloud Drive on Your Devices 94
iPhone and iPad 94
Mac 95
Windows-based PC 97
iCloud.com 98
Organizing Your Stuff 99
Creating folders 100
Managing folders and files 102

CHAPTER 10: **Picture This!** 107
Enable and Access iCloud Photos 108
iCloud.com 108
Apple devices 108
Windows-based PC 109
Working with iCloud Photos 110
iCloud.com 110
iOS 111
macOS and iPadOS 114
Windows-based PC 115

CHAPTER 11: **You've Got (iCloud) Mail** 117
Setting Up iCloud Email 118
Creating an iCloud email address 118
Accessing your iCloud email 120
Sending and Receiving Email 123
Creating and sending emails 123
Formatting emails 124
Receiving and replying to email 127

Organizing Email 128
Deleting and marking emails 128
Utilizing folders and rules 129

CHAPTER 12: **Tying a Digital String on Your Finger** 133
The Dating Game: Getting to Know Calendar 134
Accessing Calendar 134
Working with Calendar in iCloud.com 136
Remind Me, Again, Please! 141
Access Reminders 142
Working with Reminders 144

CHAPTER 13: **Noting Notes and Contacting Contacts** 153
Note to Self 154
Access Notes 154
Working with Notes 155
3 . . . 2 . . . 1 . . . Contact! 161
Access Contacts 161
Working with Contacts 162

CHAPTER 14: **Docs and Spreadsheets and Presentations, Oh My!** 167
Accessing and Working with iWork Apps 168
Using and Saving Files 170
Supported file types 170
Creating and Editing Pages Docs in iCloud 172
Managing documents 172
Working in documents 173
Working with Spreadsheets in Numbers 175
Managing spreadsheets 176
Working in spreadsheets 177
Creating Presentations in Keynote 179
Managing presentations 180
Working in presentations 181

CHAPTER 15: **Digital Lost-and-Found** 185
Enable and Access Find My 186
iCloud.com 186
Apple devices 186

On the Hunt! 187
iCloud.com 188
macOS. 190
iOS and iPadOS 190

PART 5: THE PART OF TENS. 193

CHAPTER 16: Ten Alternative Apps 195

CHAPTER 17: Ten Tips and Tricks. 199

INDEX 203

Introduction

I'm going to write something ridiculously obvious right from the start: The way we live and conduct our day-to-day ain't quite like it used to be. I remember when you had to stay in one room to use the phone, and if you got happy feet there was always the cord to remind you of your place. If you wanted to know what was going on in politics and sports, you had to read the newspaper or wait until it was time for the local and national news programs to air. I was drawn to magazine racks in grocery stores like a cat to a mouse convention; my parents never had to wonder where I was while they shopped.

Computers were cool and all, but until the early 1980s, my only experience with one was our Pong console. Pictures were taken with a camera that you had to load with film, and then you had to have the film developed before you could see that you'd cut off the top of your subject's head or that he was nearly out of the frame entirely. Calendars were something you hung on the wall and reminders and shopping lists were kept in clunky notebooks or planners. And music was something you could typically listen to only on fuzzy-sounding radios or on vinyl albums that emitted as much hiss as they did tunes. And don't get me started on the heady days when we transitioned from 8-track to cassette tapes — as someone once put it, "That's one small step for (a) man, one giant leap for mankind."

As I said, things are different now. Everything I just mentioned can now be done with a small device you can hold in the palm of your hands. Smartphones have evolved from the aforementioned handset tethered to the wall to become one of the most important tools you own. That little rectangle makes phone calls and plays music with pristine clarity. You can get the news or read magazines on it almost instantaneously. You can take stunning snapshots on a whim and share, delete, or edit them in seconds. Calendar events and reminders pop up to keep you on top of your daily activities and responsibilities. Maybe you even use your smartphone to perform your job from just about anywhere — there's no need to lug your desk along, either.

Apple is one of the companies at the forefront of these cultural upheavals. The "fruit company" that made money one less thing Forrest Gump had to worry about has arguably become the most recognizable technology brand on the planet. At first, computers drove the bottom line at Apple. Next, the iPhone and iPad had the world welcoming their sleek products into their homes and hearts. Apple then got the groovy notion that they could provide services to folks who use their devices — services such as email, cloud-based storage, productivity apps, top-notch journalism, favorite songs, movies, and TV shows, and even exercise instruction. What the heck? Let's throw video games into the mix, too!

And guess what happened? These services became popular — HUGELY so. So huge that they are now Apple's second largest revenue stream, second only to the venerable iPhone, and accounting for about 20 percent of Apple's annual income. Up until now, Apple offered these services — Music, TV+, Arcade, News+, Fitness+, and iCloud — as standalone products. Now, however, they are bundled together under the moniker Apple One. You can subscribe to Apple One at a substantially lower price than if you subscribed to each product individually.

That's where this book comes in.

About This Book

Apple One For Dummies introduces you to the Apple One ecosystem. I tell you what Apple One is, how to get it, and how it works. I discuss each of the six services included in Apple One and show you how to take advantage of all they offer, using whatever Apple device you might use for your Apple content. I even help users of non-Apple devices learn how to access Apple One products — no discrimination here. If your product supports an Apple One service, I tell you how to access and use it.

I've written this tome in such a way that you can either read it cover to cover or, if the fancy strikes you, skip around to topics that most interest you. *Dummies* books are famous for their organization, information, and levity, and I strove to bring these qualities to this book as well.

Some items in the book, such as sidebars and Technical Stuff, are simply there because I thought they were cool to know about. Just because I like them or find them interesting doesn't mean they'll be your cup of tea, so feel free to bypass them or revisit them at a later date, if you prefer.

You'll find a slew of URLs (web page addresses) that you can use to further check out the services I discuss and learn more about them. All of these URLs worked at the time of this writing, but they can change as often as a politician's opinion.

Foolish Assumptions

You rightly picked up this volume with the expectation that I, the author, had something valuable to impart regarding Apple One. However, for you to take full advantage of my expertise, I must assume a few things about your technical acumen, too.

For example, because Apple One is entirely Internet based, I must assume that you know what the Internet is. If you have no idea what I mean by the term, you might lose interest quickly as you continue reading.

Another assumption I must make is that you use at least one Apple device in your day-to-day activities. Macs, iPhones, iPads, Apple TVs, and Apple Watches are all Apple devices that will grant you purchase into the world of Apple services. Without at least one of these (preferably more), your foray into Apple One will be limited at best.

I assume you know how to successfully operate your device. If you're a seasoned user of computers, smartphones, and tablets, you should be fine, even if you're new to Apple devices. However, if the aforementioned devices are entirely foreign to you, I suggest checking out a *Dummies* title that caters to the device(s) in question before proceeding with this book.

I must also assume that you're familiar with web browsers, which are generally considered the main way to access the wonderful (and sometimes the not-so-wonderful) things the Internet has to offer. Understanding how to navigate a website and enter a URL are basics you'll want to be familiar with.

Icons Used in This Book

From time to time, you'll see one of the following icons, which will help you discern the type of topic I'm discussing.

TIP

Pay particular attention to information beside this icon. Tips are intended to help you achieve tasks being covered more easily, or may help you avoid potential snafus.

REMEMBER

Someone very close to me (sorry, I can't name names, but you know who you are) is a strong proponent of writing reminders and appointments on his or her arm and wrist with a pen. *Dummies* titles use the Remember icon to help you avoid such; just open the book and there the reminder is.

WARNING

This icon means business; don't ignore it! I use it to draw attention to potential pitfalls you may run into.

TECHNICAL STUFF

If you're a nerd like me, this icon will be a beacon for you. This information isn't necessary for you to successfully complete a task it may be associated with, but it may help you dig a bit deeper into it.

Beyond the Book

In addition to what you're reading right now, this book comes with an access-anywhere cheat sheet that provides information on how to get the most out of Siri on your Apple TV remote, as well as which browsers will give you the best experience with iCloud.com. To get the cheat sheet, simply go to `www.dummies.com` and search for *Apple One For Dummies Cheat Sheet* in the Search box.

Where to Go from Here

I've written this book with the intention that you, dear reader, would be able to approach Apple One either in the order that I've presented here or in any order you desire. No rule demands that you read this book sequentially, especially if online content services aren't new to you. However, if you are new to the concept, you may be best served to start at the beginning and work your way forward. At the very least, if you are indeed a total newb, read the chapters in Part 1 before skipping ahead.

Although I do sometimes yearn to sit back in a recliner with my newspaper, listening to vinyl records, this new digital services craze is right up my alley. The ability to access the things I love the most, or the news I want to hear, or to work from just about anywhere using the devices in my pocket or backpack is a thing of beauty to my mind. The Jetsons would be so proud of where we're headed.

1 Services, Please!

IN THIS PART . . .

Introducing Apple Services

Learning which devices you can use with Apple Services

» Discovering what each service does

» Checking out Apple One plans

Chapter 1
Getting a Handle on Apple Services

Apple's known for their capability to surprise us. Remember the small all-in-one computers that looked like lollipops on people's desks? Surprise! iMacs were a HUGE hit and helped pull Apple from the brink of obscurity. How about that little white rectangle with the circular dial on the front that held thousands of songs on it? You know, the thing Steve Jobs called an "iPod," which made you toss your CD Walkman in the trash? Surprise! Or how about the surprise of surprises: this time a black rectangle with a touchscreen that could not only hold your songs but also let you place phone calls while you surfed the web with a *real* web browser? Again, I say, surprise!

Apple's move into the multimedia market — providing music, movies, magazines, games, and the like for their legions of users (that is, fans) — wasn't exactly a surprise. But their enormous success has been. Let's find out together just what Apple services are and what they provide.

What Are Apple Services?

Apple services are not religious gatherings designed to spread the good news of the Cupertino company's wares, even though some Apple afficionados may appear to worship everything they do. In this case, these services are software platforms designed to deliver a particular set of goods to a customer.

Are you a music lover who wishes you could take all your music everywhere you go, but you don't want to clog all your devices with gigabytes of songs? Would you like to take a photo on your iPhone and instantly share it with someone across the globe? Apple can provide these types of amenities to customers through their services.

Apple's services include the following:

- Apple Music
- Apple TV+
- Apple Arcade
- Apple News+
- Apple Fitness+
- iCloud (finally, one that doesn't start with *Apple!*)

Each of these services is designed to meet a customer's needs in the simple and intuitive style Apple is known for. They're also made to work seamlessly across the spectrum of Apple's hardware devices, allowing you to move from device to device while barely skipping a beat. For example, you can watch a movie on the train after work, and then pick up right where you left off on your Apple TV the minute you walk into your apartment.

To a large extent, these services also work across non-Apple devices. Let's say you're at a friend's house working on a spreadsheet in Numbers on your iPad, but its battery dies (and, of course, you left the charger at home). No worries: Just fire up the web browser on your friend's PC, log in to iCloud.com, open Numbers from there, and get straight back to work — picking up exactly where you left off when your iPad decided to take a nap.

Now that's not just service *with* a smile but services that *cause* a smile. :)

Apple Services in a Nutshell

In this section, I introduce you to each of the aforementioned services. Getting the proverbial ten-thousand-foot view will help you get a quick idea of what each brings to the table. If you're eager to read about a particular service, feel free to flip to the chapter or chapters dedicated to it.

Apple Music

Luckily, Apple doesn't make you do much guesswork when it comes to knowing the main thrust of a service — simply read its name. Apple Music does exactly what you think it does; broadly speaking, it grants you access to music. And not just some music and not just a few select tracks. Instead you have access to lots and lots of music — to the tune (pun intended) of more than 70 million songs and counting.

Apple Music launched in 2015 and quickly gained a little over 6 million subscribers. By June 2020 those numbers were just over 70 million. Apple must be doing something right, yes?

Apple Music, shown in Figure 1-1, allows you to sync all your music across your devices even non-Apple ones, such as an Android smartphone or tablet. You can even sign into your Apple Music account in iTunes for Windows.

TIP

Apple Music is even available via your favorite web browser on just about any computer or smart device platform. Just open your browser, go to `https://music.apple.com`, and sign in to enjoy.

You can also create playlists of your favorite songs, and even listen to those curated for you by Apple based on your listening habits. Take a gander at Chapter 3 to learn all about Apple Music.

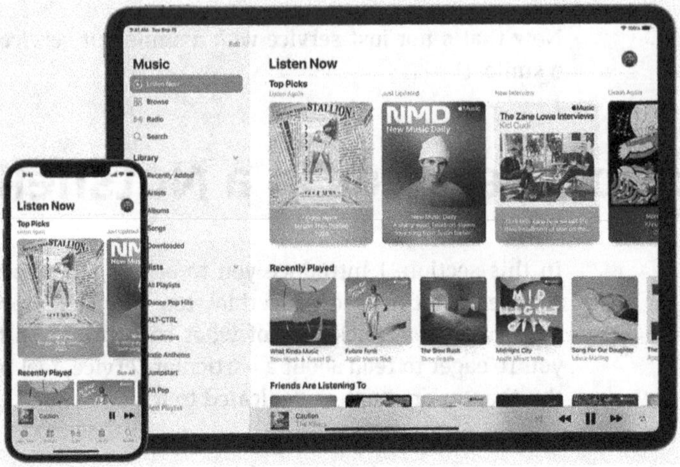

FIGURE 1-1: Apple Music works on just about any Internet-connected device.

Photo courtesy of Apple, Inc.

Apple TV+

Apple TV+ is a video streaming service that's Apple's answer to Netflix, Hulu, Amazon Prime, and the like.

Apple TV+ is relatively new to the streaming game, having been around only since the latter part of 2019. Its programming isn't as extensive as some of its toughest competitors, and consequently its user base isn't as large (around 10 million subscribers but growing).

Original programming for Apple TV+ has been outstanding, with such names as Steven Spielberg, Oprah Winfrey, and Tom Hanks (check him out in Figure 1-2) attached to the service. Apple has also been adding quality third-party content of late. One huge example of this type of programming expansion (at least in my household) is that the home of the beloved Charlie Brown specials, *A Charlie Brown Thanksgiving* and *A Charlie Brown Christmas*, is now Apple TV+, not one of the "big three" networks.

Chapter 4 discusses all things Apple TV+, including how to use it with your Apple TV streaming box.

REMEMBER The *Apple TV* moniker can be a bit confusing because it's been used for more than one product. Apple TV+ is the service we're discussing, Apple TV is the name of a hardware device, and Apple TV was the name of an app (now known as simply TV).

TED
LASSO
CENTRAL PARK

FIGURE 1-2: Apple TV+ provides great original programming.

Photo courtesy of Apple, Inc.

Apple Arcade

For years, iPhone and iPad have been great gaming devices, but no one would mistake either of them for an Xbox or a PlayStation. Games on an iPhone or iPad are fun to play and there's been a huge selection of them for quite a while. Some of the biggest games of recent years may even owe Apple a debt of gratitude for the reach into the world's households they've enjoyed; Minecraft, Angry Birds, and Fortnite leap readily to mind.

Then Apple had the wonderful notion that it would be fantastic if we could carry over gameplay from one device to another in the Apple ecosystem. You know, play your game in the car (as a passenger, of course!), and then pick up right where you left off on your Apple TV. Figure 1-3 illustrates the same game running on iPhone, iPad, Apple TV, and a Mac.

FIGURE 1-3: Apple Arcade games can easily jump from one Apple device to another.

Photo courtesy of Apple, Inc.

They then had the wonderful notion that they should provide games in a subscription format, which would cost only a small amount per month yet deliver a massive library of the latest and greatest games for their platform. Think Netflix, but for games.

Voila! Apple Arcade was born.

REMEMBER

Although some of Apple's services are available across non-Apple platforms, this is not the case with Apple Arcade. You can't take advantage of the Apple Arcade service on Android and Windows devices.

Apple News+

I mention in the Introduction how my parents always knew where they could find me: hovering around the magazine rack in our neighborhood grocery store. Back in the day (I won't say which day, to maintain some sort of mystery in the author/reader relationship), the magazine rack was where you could find at least some kind of information on just about any topic under the sun: news, sports, computers, cooking, religion, automobiles, fashion, entertainment, crosswords, and many other topics I'll save my poor tired hands from typing. Now that the Internet is the virtually unlimited source of knowledge, magazine racks have become more sparse at time goes by. (Yes, I did get a bit misty-eyed writing those words.)

Apple must have someone after my own heart working there, because I believe they saw the same distressing situation and decided to do something about it. That something is Apple News+.

Apple News+ is a virtual magazine rack, giving you online access to some of the best journalism and publications on God's green earth. Not only can you *read* the latest and greatest articles, but you can also *listen* to (many of) them, too! And Apple News+ is available on all Apple devices, including automobiles outfitted with Apple's CarPlay, shown in Figure 1-4.

Apple News+ offers entire magazines (cover to cover, no less), newspapers (local, national, and international), articles curated to your tastes, audio articles, and more. Chapter 6 gives you all the details you need to make the most of Apple News+.

9:41
Listen Now
New York City is Back in Business
The Escape
What Happened to Lee?
Churches and Saints
BACK

FIGURE 1-4: You can listen to articles on Apple News+ in your car with CarPlay.

Photo courtesy of Apple, Inc.

Apple Fitness+

Several companies deliver exercise regimens via the web, giving you access to some of the world's top trainers in your own living room. But as we all know, when Apple jumps into an existing market, they tend to not only do it well but also take it up a notch. That's what they've done with Fitness+.

Fitness+ offers video workouts by great trainers but also incorporates them into Apple's ecosystem of hardware and software catering to health and wellness. Fitness+ can offer workouts anywhere at any time and uses your Apple Watch to keep track of your body's vital health statistics before, during, and after your workouts. Those stats can be displayed onscreen (shown in Figure 1-5) using your iPhone, iPad, or Apple TV.

05:27
136
45 CAL

FIGURE 1-5: Apple Watch shows your health stats onscreen.

Photo courtesy of Apple, Inc.

REMEMBER

To use Apple Fitness+, you must have an Apple Watch (Series 3 or newer). Fitness+ is one of Apple's services that won't work with non-Apple hardware.

Chapter 7 will get you going with Apple Fitness+.

iCloud

iCloud isn't where Apple devices hang out when they die, in case you read the name of this service and envision iMacs laying on iClouds playing a harp. Rather, it's Apple's suite of online storage and productivity tools.

iCloud gets its name because Internet-based storage and other services are said to exist *in the cloud*, meaning they're not stored or installed directly on your computer or smart device.

iCloud with Apple One includes several tools:

- **iCloud Drive:** Take advantage of up to 2TB of online storage for your files. Chapter 8 shows you how to use iCloud Drive across your devices, both Apple and non-Apple.
- **Photos:** Upload and share your photos and videos across all your devices and with some of your favorite contacts (see Figure 1-6). Chapter 10 provides the details.
- **Mail:** Access your email on any device anywhere you have an Internet connection. Check out Chapter 11 to learn more on checking and sending email with your Apple email account.
- **Calendar:** Keep track of your events and subscribe to multiple calendars. Chapter 12 will help get you going.
- **Reminders:** Stay on top of the tasks you need to complete, no matter where you are. You can learn much more by perusing Chapter 12.
- **Notes:** Jot something down quickly, scan documents into iCloud, and more. Chapter 13 is waiting to give you the complete lowdown on Notes.

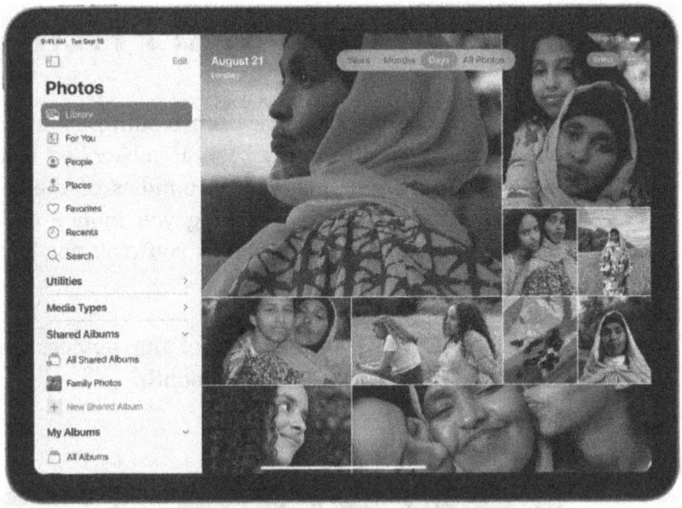
Edit
Photos
For You
People
Places
Favorites
Recents
Search
Utilities
Media Types
Shared Albums
All Shared Albums
Family Photos
New Shared Album
My Albums
All Albums
August 21

FIGURE 1-6: Photos in iCloud works on all your Internet-ready devices.

Photo courtesy of Apple, Inc.

- **Contacts:** Stay in touch with friends, family, and others by entering their contact info in Contacts. You'll want to read Chapter 13 to learn more.
- **Pages:** Create anything from a gorgeous flyer to a book with this easy-to-use but powerful word processor. Chapter 14 gives you the scoop.
- **Numbers:** Produce intuitive and informative spreadsheets and collaborate with others anywhere on the globe. See Chapter 14 for more about this app.
- **Keynote:** Make and give presentations with all the flair and style of a Steve Jobs or a Tim Cook! Chapter 14 breaks down the options and features for you.
- **Find My:** Find a lost or hiding Apple device, as long as you're signed in with your Apple ID. (I like to think that mine hide rather than that I lost them.) Chapter 15 will become your best friend once you learn how to find your lost (or hiding) devices.

Chapter 8 will help you get a handle on how iCloud works and how you can access its awesome array of tools.

Apple One Plans and Pricing

Each of the services you've been reading about would cost a pretty penny on a monthly basis if subscribed to individually. Apple One lets you subscribe to bundles of these services for a substantially lower rate, saving you money and potentially introducing you to some services you may not have otherwise taken advantage of.

Table 1-1 provides an overview of the services included with each plan, as well as pricing per month.

TABLE 1-1 Apple One Plans

Service	Individual ($14.95/ Month)	Family ($19.95/ Month)	Premier ($29.95/ Month
Apple Music	Yes	Yes	Yes
Apple TV+	Yes	Yes	Yes
Apple Arcade	Yes	Yes	Yes
iCloud	Up to 50GB	Up to 200GB	Up to 2TB
Apple News+	No	No	Yes
Apple Fitness+	No	No	Yes

The Individual plan will save you $6 per month ($72 per year) over subscribing to each service separately. The Family plan saves you $8 per month ($96 a year), and the Premier plan saves $25 a month, or a great big $300 a year!

IN THIS CHAPTER

» Finding out which devices you can use

» Learning about and updating operating systems

» Discovering supported web browsers

Chapter 2 Cool Devices for Cool Services

Now that you've learned what Apple One offers and just how freaking awesome it is, it's time to discover the kinds of devices Apple One services will work with. Since Apple One is an Apple product, it stands to reason that Apple devices are the best ones to use with its services. However, you're not limited to *only* Apple devices. For example, some Apple One services are available via a web browser, which means you can access them on just about any Internet-connected device. Another example is Apple Music, which offers an app for Android smartphones and tablets.

In this chapter, you learn more about how you can use your computer, smartphone, or tablet to enjoy Apple One's services.

Finding Devices Ready for Apple One

One of the perks of Apple One is that many of its features are available via various hardware and software avenues. However, to get started with Apple One, you must have an Apple device.

In this section, I discuss which devices will work with Apple One services and how to make sure their operating system software is up to date.

WARNING

It's my very strong opinion (having wrecked entire weekends by not doing so) that you should always — and I mean ALWAYS — back up any device that you're about to upgrade. This advice is especially important if you're upgrading the operating system of a device, computer or otherwise. Sometimes operating system upgrades incorporate major changes in the way you work with your device and software applications you've installed. The best way to avoid a monumental disaster if things go awry is to have a backup of your important items. Please check with your device's manufacturer for the best ways to back it up. I also recommend backing up before signing up for Apple One, just to be sure things like your Music library are saved in case you have any issues (however unlikely) merging your files with these services.

iPhone

The iPhone is the device that opened the world to Apple. Sure, people knew of Apple, but most hadn't used an Apple product until Steve Jobs announced this shiny new object in 2007. Its allure was simply too much for folks to resist (guilty!), and it's now a staple of life and culture — truly a life-altering technological innovation.

WHAT IS AN OPERATING SYSTEM?

Operating systems are to computers, smartphones, and tablets what engines are to automobiles. They're what makes the thing go. An operating system (OS) is software that allows you to interact with your computer or smart device. You tell the OS that you want to perform a task by clicking, moving, saying, or tapping something. The OS then tells the your device hardware what you want it to do, such as shut down, restart, play a music file, make a phone call, or what-have-you. Not all devices run the same OS, as you discover in this chapter, but thankfully, these days most will work together at least on some level and are similar enough in their functionality that if you can use one you can quickly learn another.

All Apple One services are available to iPhone users, but you'll need something a bit newer than the 2007 model I just mentioned. Your iPhone must be able to run at least iOS 14 to subscribe to and use Apple One's services. iOS 14 is supported on the following iPhone models:

- iPhone 12, 12 mini, 12 Pro, and 12 Pro Max
- iPhone 11, 11 Pro, and 11 Pro Max
- iPhone Xs and Xs Max
- iPhone XR
- iPhone X
- iPhone 8 and 8 Plus
- iPhone 7 and 7 Plus
- iPhone 6S and 6S Plus
- iPhone SE, 1st and 2nd generations

TIP

Visit Apple's support site at `https://support.apple.com` if you need help determining your iPhone model.

It's a good idea to make sure your device is running the latest and greatest version of its OS. To check the iOS on your iPhone, do the following:

1. **Tap the gear icon (Settings).**
2. **Tap General and then tap Software Update.**

   Your iPhone checks to see if any updates are available. If so, they appear in the Software Update window (shown in Figure 2-1).

   TIP

   It's a good idea — and sometimes required if the battery is low — to connect your iPhone to a charger during an update.

3. **To download and install the update to your iPhone, tap Download and Install.**

   Your iPhone will restart at least once during the process, so don't be alarmed when it does.

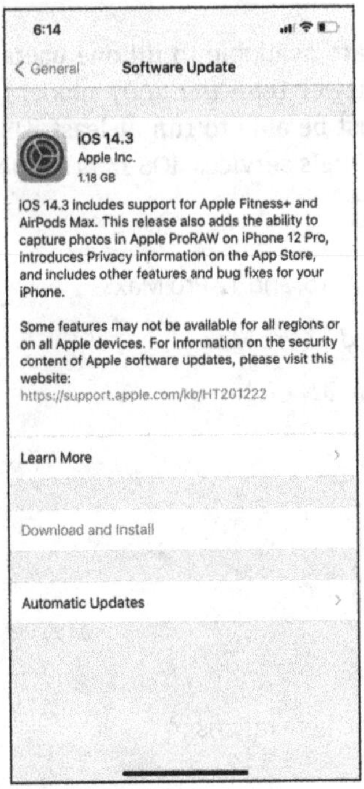
6:14
General
Software Update
iOS 14.3
Apple Inc.
1.18 GB
iOS 14.3 includes support for Apple Fitness+ and AirPods Max. This release also adds the ability to capture photos in Apple ProRAW on iPhone 12 Pro, introduces Privacy information on the App Store, and includes other features and bug fixes for your iPhone.
Some features may not be available for all regions or on all Apple devices. For information on the security content of Apple software updates, please visit this website:
https://support.apple.com/kb/HT201222
Learn More
Download and Install
Automatic Updates

FIGURE 2-1: If updates are available, you'll see them here.

iPad

iPads are the iPhone's nearest cousin. They really do function as much larger versions of an iPhone, but without the capability to make phone calls (although they can make FaceTime video calls quite nicely). Even the OS that they run, iPadOS, is a spin-off from iOS. You'll need iPadOS 14 to sign up for Apple One services. iPads that support iPadOS 14 are as follows:

- iPad Pro 12.9-inch (1st, 2nd, 3rd, and 4th generations)
- iPad Pro 11-inch (1st and 2nd generations)
- iPad Pro 10.5-inch
- iPad Pro 9.7-inch
- iPad (5th, 6th, 7th, and 8th generations)
- iPad mini (5th generation)

- iPad mini 4
- iPad Air (3rd and 4th generations)
- iPad Air 2

TIP

Check Apple's support site at `https://support.apple.com` if you need help finding out which iPad model you have.

To make sure your iPad is running the latest version of iPadOS, do the following:

1. **Tap the Settings icon (gear).**
2. **Tap General and then tap Software Update.**

   Your iPad checks to see if any updates available. If so, they appear in the Software Update window.
3. **To download and install the update to your iPad, tap Download and Install.**

   Your iPad will restart at least once during the process.

Mac

The Mac, Apple's version of a personal computer, is most decidedly not made to work in the same manner as an iPhone or iPad. Macs come in several varieties: iMacs (all-in-one desktop computers), MacBooks (laptops), Mac minis (small no-frills boxes that require users to supply their own monitor, keyboard, and mouse), and Mac Pro (large high-end desktop computers for which the user must provide a monitor).

The Mac is a traditional computer, using a keyboard and a mouse or trackpad for navigation. Its operating system, macOS, is quite different than that of the iPhone or iPad due to the differences in interfaces. The latest version of macOS is called Big Sur (Apple can get creative with their macOS names), and you'll need to be running it on your Mac to sign up for Apple One services.

TECHNICAL STUFF

For help finding out which macOS version you're currently running, and determining which version number it is, check out this site on Apple's Support page: `https://support.apple.com/en-us/HT201260`.

Mac models that support macOS Big Sur follow:

- » iMac (2014 model or later)
- » iMac Pro (2017 or later)
- » Mac Pro (2013 or later)
- » Mac mini (2014 or later)
- » MacBook Air (2013 or later)
- » MacBook Pro (late 2013 and later)
- » MacBook (2015 and later)

TIP

Visit Apple's support site at `https://support.apple.com` if you need help determining your Mac model.

To upgrade your Mac to the latest macOS, do the following:

1. **Click the icon in the upper-left corner of your screen and choose System Preferences.**
2. **Locate and click Software Update.**

   Your Mac will check to see if any updates are available. If so, they appear in the Software Update window, as shown in Figure 2-2.

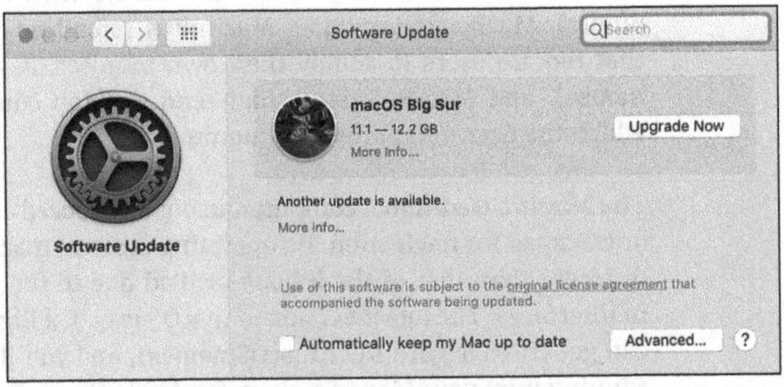

Software Update
Search
macOS Big Sur
11.1 — 12.2 GB
More Info...
Upgrade Now
Another update is available.
More info...
Software Update
Use of this software is subject to the original license agreement that accompanied the software being updated.
Automatically keep my Mac up to date
Advanced...
?

FIGURE 2-2: It looks like it's time for me to upgrade to macOS Big Sur.

3. **To download the file, click the Upgrade Now button.**

   The file is large, so it may take a while to download. The installer opens automatically when the file finishes downloading.

4. **Click Continue and follow the onscreen instructions.**

   You can expect your Mac to restart at least once during the upgrade.

Apple TV

You're not alone if the name Apple TV throws you off; several people have been surprised hearing the name "Apple TV," thinking that Apple makes televisions. Rather, Apple TV is a small box (seen in Figure 2-3) that uses Apple software to stream content from the Internet to your television via a single HDMI cable.

tv
MENU

FIGURE 2-3: Apple TV is a small device that delivers big entertainment.

Image courtesy of Apple, Inc.

Apple currently has two versions of the diminutive dynamo, Apple TV 4K and Apple TV HD, and both are quite capable of meeting your streaming needs. Because Apple TV is a type of computer, it must run an operating system, in this case, tvOS. tvOS 14 is the newest version, and it is required to subscribe to Apple One services from your Apple TV.

To make sure your Apple TV is running the latest tvOS, grab your Apple TV remote and follow these instructions:

1. **Click the Settings app on the Apple TV home screen.**
2. **Click System ⇨ Software Updates ⇨ Update Software.**

   Apple TV queries Apple's servers to find out if an update is available. If so, it appears on the screen.
3. **Click Download and Install.**

   Your Apple TV downloads the update file and begins the installation process. It restarts twice during this time.

WARNING

Be sure not to unplug or disconnect your Apple TV while it's updating, or things could get ugly. If your Apple TV becomes disconnected or unplugged during updating and won't start correctly, reach out to Apple Support for help: `https://support.apple.com/apple-tv`.

Apple Watch

Apple Watch is not required to subscribe to Apple One services, but it is required to use one of the services: Fitness+. Fitness+ captures important information about your health during your workouts, such as your heart rate and blood oxygen levels. You can also use it to select various types of workouts right from your wrist.

watchOS is the name of the Apple Watch's operating system. (Have you noticed a pattern with Apple's naming conventions yet?) Fitness+ requires you to be running at least watchOS 7 to take advantage of its innovative workouts. The following Apple Watch models support watchOS 7:

- Apple Watch Series 6
- Apple Watch Series SE
- Apple Watch Series 5
- Apple Watch Series 4
- Apple Watch Series 3

TIP

Visit Apple's Support site at https://support.apple.com/en-us/HT204507 for help in finding out which Apple Watch model you have.

To update your Apple Watch to the latest watchOS version, do the following:

1. **Connect your Apple Watch to its charger.**
2. **Check to be sure your Apple Watch is connected to Wi-Fi.**

   It won't update via cellular, even if you have a cellular model.
3. **Open the Settings app on your Apple Watch.**
4. **Tap General, and then tap Software Update, as shown in Figure 2-4.**
5. **If an update is available, tap Install and follow the onscreen prompts to complete the update.**

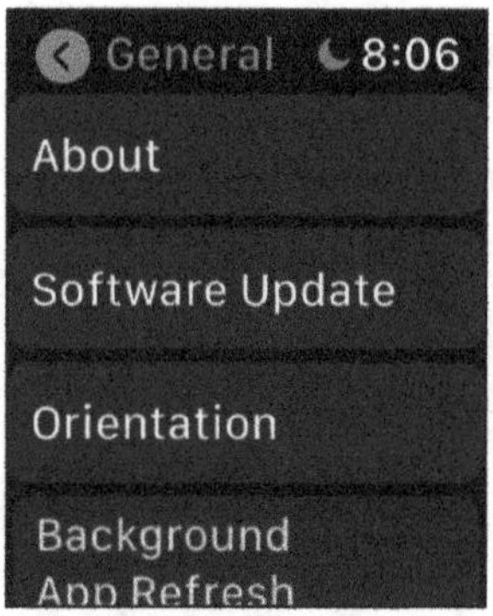
General
8:06
About
Software Update
Orientation
Background

FIGURE 2-4: Tap Software Update to see if a watchOS update is ready.

You can update your Apple Watch also by using the Watch app on your iPhone. Your iPhone must be running the latest version of iOS to perform this update and must be connected to Wi-Fi (cellular won't do). Your Apple Watch must be at least 50 percent charged. For further instructions, check out https://support.apple.com/en-us/HT204641.

PCs

Yes, Windows users, you, too, can experience the thrills of Apple One! You need to have at least one of the Apple devices mentioned in this chapter to subscribe to Apple One, but after that you can take advantage of several services.

Apple offers Windows-native apps for a few Apple One services: Apple Music (via iTunes for Windows) and iCloud. Other services may be accessed using a modern and updated web browser (more on that later in this chapter). To use these apps, it's best that your Windows installation is up to date.

Windows 10 users can download and install these apps quite easily:

1. **Launch the Microsoft Store.**

   The Microsoft Store window appears.

2. **Click Search in the upper-right corner, type** Apple, **and press Enter.**

3. **Scroll to the Apps section.**

   Two apps you'll find are iTunes and iCloud, as shown in Figure 2-5.

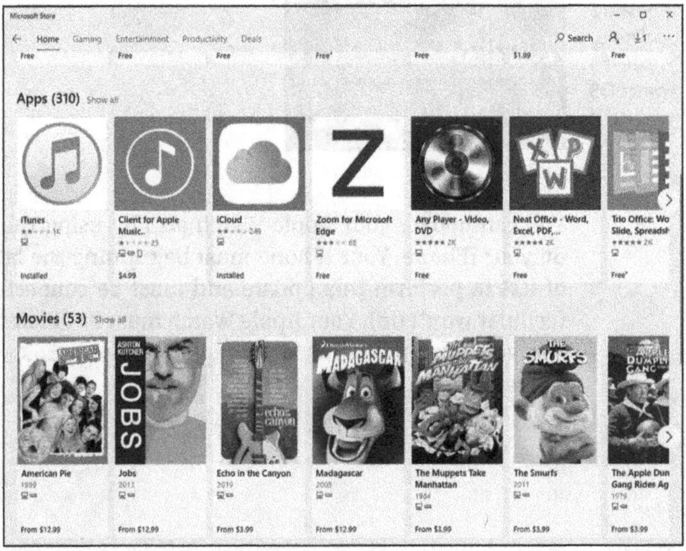
Microsoft Store
Home
Gaming
Entertainment
Productivity
Deals
Search
Apps (310)
iTunes
Client for Apple Music..
iCloud
Zoom for Microsoft Edge
Any Player - Video, DVD
Neat Office - Word, Excel, PDF,...
Movies (53)
American Pie
Jobs
Echo in the Canyon
Madagascar
The Muppets Take Manhattan
The Smurfs

FIGURE 2-5: iTunes and iCloud are available for Windows.

4. **To see information about an app, click it.**
5. **To install the app, select it (if necessary) and click the Get button.**

   The app automatically launches after the installation process is complete.

TIP

Apple also provides the Apple TV app for Xbox One and Xbox Series X|S users through the Microsoft Store on those devices.

Windows 7 and 8 users are also able to install iTunes and iCloud for their OS. For iTunes go to `https://support.apple.com/en-us/HT210384`, and for iCloud visit `https://support.apple.com/en-us/HT204283`. Be sure to look for the downloads for your version of Windows.

TIP

Sorry Linux fans, but Apple doesn't provide any native apps to use with Apple One services. However, you can take advantage of some of them through your favorite web browser. Check out the upcoming section, "Apple One on the WWW."

Android

In some circles of geekdom, Android and Apple users go together like Fruity Pebbles and marinara. Not here, dear reader! We're all one happy family in these parts, and I won't steer you wrong if you're looking to use Apple One services on your Android devices.

Apple offers one native Android app for Apple Music, but I'm afraid that's it for now. You'll want to make sure that the OS on your Android device is up to date before downloading and installing the Apple Music app from the Google Play Store. However, you can use a web browser to access many of the other Apple One services on Android devices. Keep reading to learn more.

Apple One on the WWW

Don't get down in the dumps if you didn't see your favorite device listed in the previous section. Because Apple One services are Internet-based, most can be accessed through the ever-expanding World Wide Web on your favorite web browser.

Just about any Internet-connected device — whether computer, smartphone, or tablet — comes with a web browser, and if the one that's built-in doesn't suit you, you can almost be assured there's another one you can download and install that you'll like better.

Although you can access many Apple One services from a web browser, some functionality may be limited. For example, the way you interact with iCloud Drive differs in a web browser (via iCloud.com) than it does in the Files app on an iPhone, and some features may not be available.

These Apple One services are accessible with a web browser:

- Apple Music (`https://music.apple.com`)
- Apple TV (`https://tv.apple.com`), shown running in Google Chrome for Windows in Figure 2-6
- iCloud (`https://icloud.com`), which includes Mail, Contacts, Calendar, Photos, iCloud Drive, Notes, Reminders, Pages, Numbers, Keynote, Find Friends, and Find iPhone

Apple News+, Arcade, and Fitness+ all require Apple devices.

Supported web browsers include the following:

- Safari (macOS, iOS, and iPadOS)
- Google Chrome (macOS, iOS, iPadOS, Windows, Android, and Linux)
- Mozilla Firefox (macOS, iOS, iPadOS, Windows, Android, and Linux)

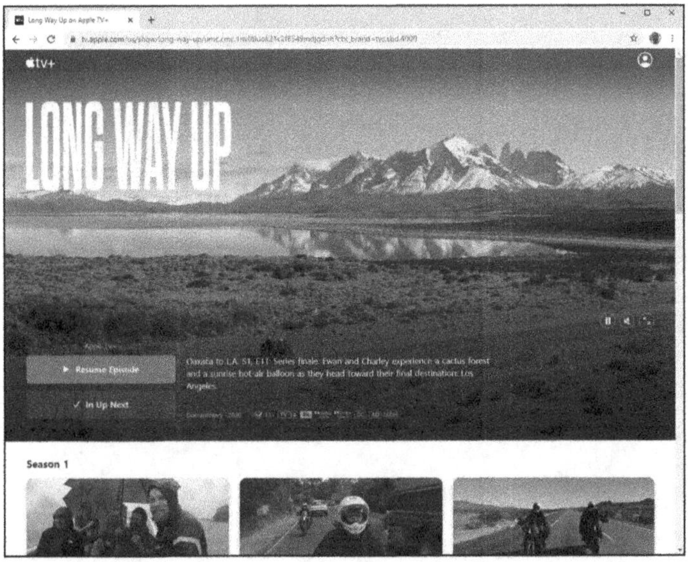
LONG WAY UP
Season 1

FIGURE 2-6: Enjoying *Long Way Up* on Apple TV+ using Chrome for Windows.

- » Microsoft Edge (Windows)
- » Brave (macOS, iOS, iPadOS, Windows, Android, and Linux)
- » Opera (macOS, iOS, iPadOS, Windows, Android, and Linux)

REMEMBER

Other browsers may work, but please don't hold my feet to the fire if you try one and things get a bit wonky.

As the adage goes, there's more than one way to skin a cat (who in the world came up with that?), or in this case, to get to your Apple One services. Upcoming chapters tackle how to access the features or individual services across their supported platforms.

2

Are You Not Entertained?

IN THIS PART . . .

Listening to your favorite tunes anywhere with Music

Discovering new shows and movies on Apple TV+

Playing games with Apple Arcade

IN THIS CHAPTER

» Accessing Apple Music on your devices

» Finding your favorite tunes

Chapter 3

Get Yo Groove On

This chapter takes its title from the 1996 song by Prince, which you can listen to using Apple's Music app (or website) on your computer, smartphone, or tablet. Of course, your Apple One subscription is what makes this and thousands of other songs available to you on just about any Internet-connected device you own. Apple Music streams tunes into your life that are already your favorites and also lets you discover great artists and titles you didn't even know existed. "Get Yo Groove On" is a perfect example of a great, mostly unknown song (performed by a musical legend) that's available through one of Apple's most popular services.

Apple Music is a part of all three Apple One subscription levels, so you can crank up some jams regardless of which plan you go with. It's accessible also on non-Apple devices, which only serves to broaden its appeal. As long as you're signed in using the same Apple ID, your favorites and history will follow you whichever device you use.

REMEMBER

Apple Music is a premium music subscription service and Music is the app used to listen to that music. From this point, I refer to *Music* when discussing the app and actions you make in it and *Apple Music* when talking about the subscription plan.

Access Apple Music

You'll need to be signed into your Apple ID on the devices you want to use with your Apple Music subscription. After you do that, the Music app will be your ticket to music paradise.

TIP

Back up the music files on your computer or smart device before you access Apple Music on them. Although a major hiccup is rare, it's best to be prepared.

iPhone and iPad

The Music app is installed with every iPhone and iPad by default. You can find it on the Home screen by its easily recognizable musical note icon.

Start by looking at some settings options, and then you launch the app:

1. **Open the Settings app.**
2. **Ensure that you're logged in to your Apple ID.**

   If you don't see your name at the top of the Settings list, tap Sign In and sign in with your Apple ID username and password.
3. **Swipe down the Settings list and tap Music.**

   Several options are available, but two are most important when getting started with the Music app.
4. **Change the following options, if desired:**
   - *Sync Library:* If you'd like to synchronize your musical content across all your devices, toggle the Sync Library switch to On (green). This syncs songs you add to or delete from your library while using Apple Music, songs you purchase, and songs you import.
   - *Cellular Data:* Tap this option and then toggle the Cellular Data switch to On (green) if you want to use your cellular data plan to download and listen to songs in the Music app. If you disable this option, you'll be able to download and listen to songs only when your device is connected to Wi-Fi.

TIP

If you don't have an unlimited cellular data plan and intend to use the Music app quite heavily with Apple Music streaming, disabling the Cellular Data option is a good idea. By limiting your download and streaming playback to only when connected to Wi-Fi, you could be saving yourself from a large bill from your cellular service provider.

5. **Leave the Settings app.**

   If your iPhone or iPad uses Face ID, swipe up. If your iPhone or iPad has a Home button, press it.

6. **Tap to open the Music app and begin jamming.**

Mac

Like Music for iOS and iPadOS, Music comes installed by default on all Macs through macOS. The app sports the same iconic musical note logo, making it easy to distinguish.

Open Music and ensure that you're signed in to your Apple Music subscription.

1. **Click the Music icon in the dock to launch the app.**

   If you don't see the icon in the dock, you'll find it in your Applications folder.

2. **Choose Account ⇨ Sign In from the menu at the top of the screen.**

3. **Type your Apple ID username and password, and then click Sign In.**

   Now you're signed into your Apple Music subscription and can begin enjoying your songs.

Windows

Yep, you read that right — Apple Music is available for Windows computers. However, the app you'll use to access your Apple Music subscription is iTunes, not the Music app you may be using on your Apple devices.

To set up iTunes for Windows and sign in to your Apple Music subscription:

1. **Open the Microsoft Store in Windows 10, search for iTunes, and install it.**

   If you have Windows 7 or 8, download iTunes from `www.apple.com/itunes/download/`.

2. **Select the Start menu and click iTunes from the apps list to launch it.**

3. **Select Account ⇨ Sign In from the menu at the top of the window.**

   You're now signed into your Apple Music subscription and can start rockin' with your PC!

Android

Just as surprising as finding out that Apple supports Windows for Apple Music streaming is the fact that subscribers can also use their Android devices. I'm kinda proud of Apple for reaching across the aisle like this! When you have something great going on, I guess it's a good idea to make sure you can reach as many folks as possible, huh?

TIP

You'll need an Android phone or tablet running at least Android 5.0 (Lollipop) to download and install Apple's Music app.

To set up the Music app for Android and sign into your Apple Music subscription:

1. **Download the Apple Music app from the Google Play Store.**

   TIP

   Don't confuse the name of the Android version of the app, Apple Music, with the streaming service. In this step you're only downloading the app, not signing into your subscription.

2. **Do the following:**
   - *If you see an offer for a free trial:* Tap Sign In in the upper-right corner of the app.
   - *If you don't see an offer for a free trial:* Tap the More button (three red dots) and then tap Sign In.

3. **Enter your Apple ID username and password.**

   Now you're signed into your Apple Music subscription and can start cranking out some tunes.

Website

Don't have any of the previous operating systems or devices? Unable to install the Music or iTunes app? No worries — Apple also offers Music as a website that you can access from any Internet-capable device on the globe.

To access Apple Music through the Music website:

1. **Open your favorite web browser on any Internet-capable device.**

   TIP

   I recommend using the most up-to-date version of the browser. It's also a good idea to stick to one of the more popular browsers (Safari, Chrome, Firefox, or Edge) to ensure proper playback compatibility.

2. **Click or tap the Sign In button in the upper-right corner of the browser window.**
3. **Type your Apple ID username and click or tap the arrow.**
4. **Type your Apple ID password and click or tap the arrow to sign in to your subscription.**

   Now you're signed into your Apple Music subscription and can play whatever floats your boat at the moment.

Groovin' with Your Tunes

The Music app is designed to work much the same regardless of the device you're using, but because some use touchscreens and others use a more traditional point-and-click interface with a mouse or trackpad, certain features and options are found in different places.

iPhone, iPad, and Android

iPhones, iPads, and Android devices all use a touchscreen (for the most part) to interact with their apps, so the Music app looks and behaves similarly on them all. Figure 3-1 shows you how to navigate Music for touchscreen devices.

Account info
2:22
Listen Now
Top Picks
Featuring Simple Minds
Music
Simple Minds & Similar Artists Station
'80s
Recently Played
See All
Hang On To Your Love
Tabs bar
Current song

FIGURE 3-1: The Music app playing some notes on an iPhone.

Tap an icon at the bottom of the screen to see what the Music app offers:

- **Listen Now:** Find recommendations based on your listening patterns and preferences. Swipe up and down to find several categories that may cater to your fancy.
- **Browse:** See what's hot in Apple Music. Find various charts and playlists that help you discover new music and rediscover old favorites.
- **Radio:** Apple Music subscribers will see a bevy of Internet radio stations that play anything from oldies to the newest tracks. Find radio shows by topic, artist, musical genres, and more.
- **Library:** Peruse your library of songs, both those you own and store on your device and those stored in the Apple Music cloud.
- **Search:** Tap the Search icon, tap the Search field at the top of the window, and then tap either the Apple Music tab or the Your Library tab under the Search field to find songs in one or the other location.

  TIP

  Your library is for songs that you physically store on your device.

Figure 3-2 shows you the lay of the land when viewing an album.

A couple of options bear a bit more explanation:

- **More icon:** Tap here to share the album with others, mark it as an album you love or don't fancy (to assist Apple Music in curating your tastes), add it to your library, make a playlist from it, and more.
- **Current song playbar:** Tap to open the songs playback window, shown in Figure 3-3.

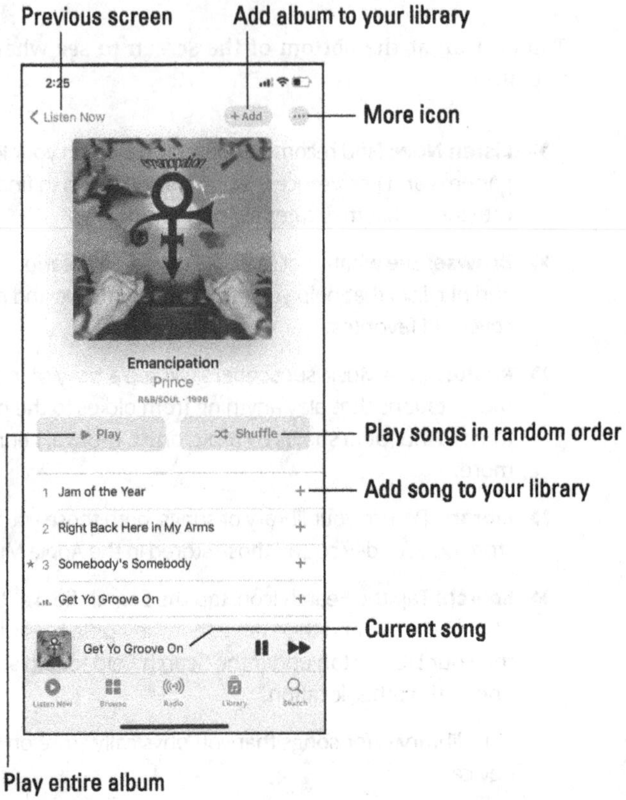
Previous screen
Add album to your library
More icon
Listen Now
+ Add
Emancipation
Prince
Play
Shuffle
Play songs in random order
Jam of the Year
Right Back Here in My Arms
Somebody's Somebody
Get Yo Groove On
Add song to your library
Current song
Play entire album

FIGURE 3-2: Viewing an album in Music on a touchscreen.

Figure 3-3 is your guide to navigating the currently playing song. Let's take a closer look at some of these options:

- **More icon:** Tap here to share the song with others, mark it as like or don't like (to assist Apple Music in curating your tastes), add it to your library, make a playlist from it, create a radio station based off of it, and more.
- **Playhead:** Drag the playhead to a position in the song.
- **View Lyrics:** Tap to view a song's lyrics on the screen.
- **AirPlay:** Tap to play the song on a nearby Apple TV, Apple HomePod, or other AirPlay-compatible device.
- **Volume slider:** Drag to adjust the volume of the song.

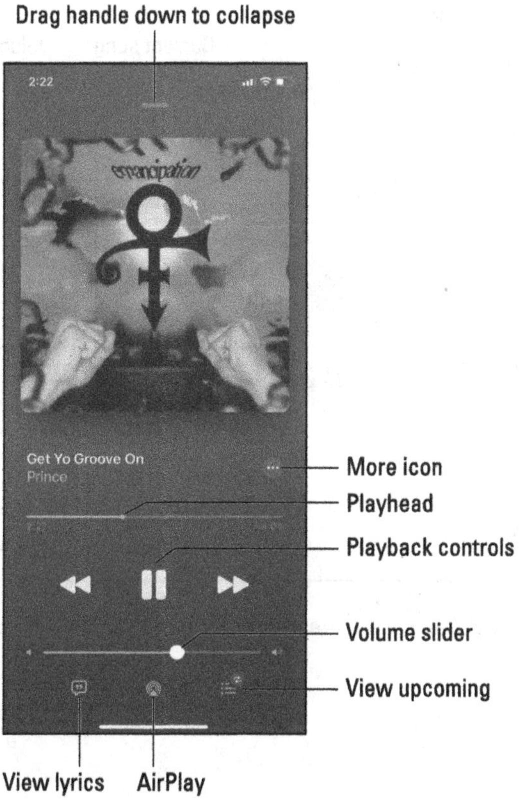
Drag handle down to collapse
2:22
Get Yo Groove On
Prince
More icon
Playhead
Playback controls
Volume slider
View upcoming
View lyrics
AirPlay

FIGURE 3-3: Playing a song in Music on an iPhone.

Mac, Windows, and Website

Music for Mac, iTunes for Windows, and the Music website all function much the same. Figure 3-4 shows you how to play your favorite tracks on your computer.

Let's take a closer look at some of these options:

- » **Playhead:** Drag the playhead to a position in the song.
- » **Sidebar:** Select an item in the sidebar to view and play related music. The sidebar gives you access to your Apple Music subscription, playlists, and more.

Check out Apple's Music Support site for much information on topics such as downloading songs to your device, purchasing music, and more: `https://support.apple.com/music`.

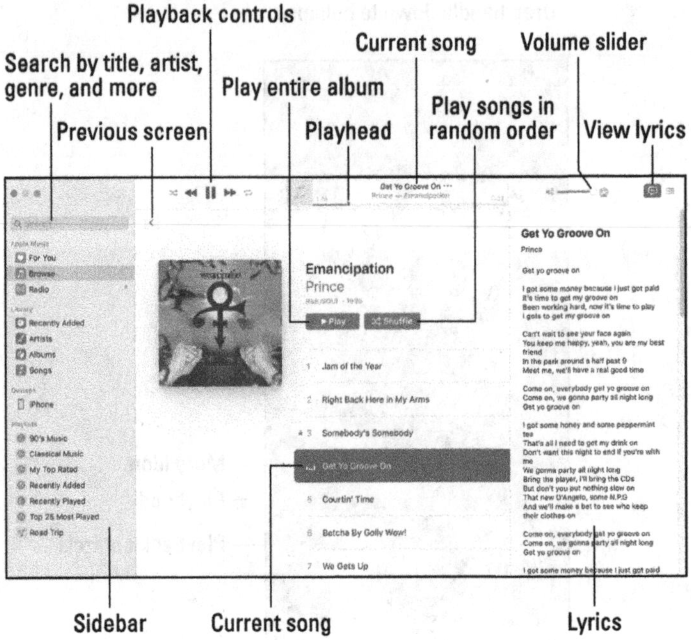
Playback controls
Current song
Volume slider
Search by title, artist, genre, and more
Play entire album
Play songs in random order
Previous screen
Playhead
View lyrics
Get Yo Groove On
Prince
Emancipation
Prince
Play
Shuffle
Jam of the Year
Right Back Here in My Arms
Somebody's Somebody
Get Yo Groove On
Courtin' Time
Betcha By Golly Wow!
We Gets Up
For You
Browse
Radio
Recently Added
Artists
Albums
Songs
iPhone
90's Music
Classical Music
My Top Rated
Recently Added
Recently Played
Top 25 Most Played
Road Trip
Sidebar
Current song
Lyrics

FIGURE 3-4: Music on a Mac works much like iTunes on Windows and Music on the web.

» Finding something good to watch

» Downloading content to watch offline

Chapter 4

Not Just TV — TV+!

My, how television has changed! I used to be the remote control for my grandfather, and now I can control my own TV from my watch. Now that's progress! And instead of having only three channels (and maybe a fourth on a sunny day), endless options are available on live television and multiple streaming platforms. You can watch television all day long just about anywhere you are, and you'll never run out of options.

Apple has provided streaming content from other providers for years through the iTunes Store, and you could watch that content on the TV app (formerly known as Videos). Apple's first in-house foray into the streaming market was Apple TV, a device that connects to your television, pumping content to it from all over the Internet. Apple then created Apple TV+ and quickly began producing an award-winning lineup of shows and movies (Apple Originals).

In this chapter, you find out how to take advantage of your Apple One subscription to enjoy streaming content from Apple and other platforms on your devices, even non-Apple ones.

REMEMBER

Apple TV+ is the premium subscription service, Apple TV is a streaming device, and TV is an app developed by Apple used to view your Apple TV+ movies and shows on various Apple devices.

Access Apple TV+

You'll need to be signed into your Apple ID on the devices you want to use with your Apple TV+ subscription. After that, you'll be able to enjoy your Apple TV+ content anywhere you have an Internet connection (and even sometimes when you don't).

iPhone and iPad

The TV app is installed on every iPhone and iPad by default. You can find it on the Home screen by looking for its distinctive tv icon.

First you look at some settings options, and then you launch the Apple TV app:

1. **Open the Settings app.**
2. **Ensure that you're logged in to your Apple ID.**

   If you're signed in, you'll see your name at the top of the Settings list. If you don't see your name, tap Sign In and sign in with your Apple ID username and password.
3. **Swipe down the Settings list and tap TV.**

   Several options are available. I cover the most important ones when getting started with the app.
4. **Do the following:**
   - *Video Definition:* Tap this option and select either High Definition (HD) or Standard Definition (SD) for the resolution of the videos you rent or purchase from your iPhone or iPad. HD videos look great but take up much more storage space than SD. If storage is a concern, consider just going with SD for this option. The difference in appearance isn't that significant on the smaller screens of iPhones and iPads.
   - *Cellular Data:* Tap this option in the Streaming Options section, the Download Options section, or both, and then toggle the Cellular Data switch to On (green) if you want to use your cellular data plan to download and listen to movies and shows in the Apple TV app.

TIP

If you disable the Cellular Data options, you'll be able to download and view streaming content only when your device is connected to Wi-Fi, which is a good thing if you don't have an unlimited cellular data plan.

5. **Leave the Settings app.**

   If your iPhone or iPad uses Face ID, swipe up. If your device has a Home button, press it.

6. **Tap to open the TV app.**

Mac

Your Mac also comes with the TV app preinstalled, and sports the same tv logo to help you spot it easily.

To open the Apple TV app and ensure that you're signed in to your Apple TV+ subscription:

1. **Click the TV icon in the dock to launch the app.**

   If for some reason you don't see it there, you'll find it in your Applications folder.

2. **Choose Account ⇨ Sign In from the menu at the top of the screen.**

3. **Type your Apple ID username and password, and then click Sign In.**

   Now you're signed into your Apple TV+ subscription and can binge-watch to your heart's desire.

Apple TV

The Apple TV streaming device is a small black box that places an immense amount of entertainment in your hands via its innovative remote control. Our family has had one since they were introduced and have kept at least one in the house ever since. There's no more user-friendly and elegant way to find and play streaming content, in my humble opinion.

Apple TV utilizes apps much like your iPhone, iPad, and Mac do. There's even an app store that you use to download apps from other streaming providers, such as Netflix, Hulu, Disney+, and Amazon Prime.

TIP

When you first set up your Apple TV, you'll be prompted to sign in with your Apple ID. However, if for some reason you've signed out of it or have multiple Apple IDs, please continue with the following steps.

To make sure you're signed into your Apple TV+ subscription and then to open the TV app:

1. **Click the Settings app on your Apple TV's Home screen using your remote control.**
2. **Select Users and Accounts, and then select Add New User.**
3. **Type your Apple ID username and password, and then click Sign In.**
4. **Press the Menu key on your remote control until you get back to the Home screen, and then click the TV app icon.**

   You're ready to start watching Apple Originals and other streaming content using your little black box.

TIP

To find out more about the various Apple TV models, visit `www.apple.com/tv/`.

Smart TVs and gaming consoles

Certain smart TVs and gaming consoles support the Apple TV app. You can download the app from your TV or console app store, and then sign in with your Apple ID to access your Apple TV+ subscription from them.

Samsung, LG, VIZIO, and Sony make smart TVs that support Apple TV. For more information, visit `https://support.apple.com/en-gw/guide/tvplus/apd903e39682/1.0/web/1.0`.

As for gaming consoles, Xbox and PlayStation are the kings of the hill, and they both support the Apple TV app, as well. To find out how to install and sign in to the Apple TV app on these platforms, check out https://support.apple.com/en-gw/guide/tvplus/apdae97576f2/1.0/web/1.0.

Non-Apple streaming devices

Apple doesn't want to alienate fans who happen to have a non-Apple streaming device, so they've thoughtfully developed the Apple TV app to work with three of the most popular: Roku, Amazon Fire TV, and Google TV.

Each platform has their way of doing things, so take a gander at https://support.apple.com/en-gw/guide/tvplus/apd2d7fd79ba/1.0/web/1.0 to find out how to install and sign in to the Apple TV app on your device.

Website

Are you unable to install the Apple TV app or don't use a supported operating system or device? Apple has you covered with the Apple TV website, which you can access from any Internet-capable device.

To access your Apple TV+ subscription through the Apple TV website:

1. **Open your favorite web browser on any Internet-capable device.**
2. **Click or tap the Sign In button in the upper-right corner of the browser window.**
3. **Type your Apple ID username and then click or tap the arrow.**
4. **Type your Apple ID password and then click or tap the arrow to sign into your subscription.**

   Enjoy your favorite movies and shows anywhere anytime.

Watching Your Apple Gogglebox

The Apple TV app is designed to work much the same regardless of the device you're using, but since some use touchscreens and others use a more traditional point-and-click interface with a mouse or trackpad, some features and options are found in different places.

iPhone and iPad

The Apple TV app works much the same on iOS and iPadOS. Figure 4-1 shows you how to navigate Apple TV for iPhone and iPad.

2:25
Library
Movies
The Lord of the Rings: T...
The Lord of the Rings: T...
The Lord of the Rings: T...
Mad Max: Fury Road
A Man for All Seasons (1...
Midnight in Paris
North By Northwest
Of Gods and Men (Subtit...
Sabrina (1995)
Schindler's List
Watch Now
Originals
Library
Search

FIGURE 4-1: Checking out my library in the Apple TV app for iOS.

Tap a tab at the bottom of the screen to explore the Apple TV app options:

- **Watch Now:** Find recommendations based on your watching history and see the newest offerings from content providers. Swipe up and down to find several categories that interest you.
- **Originals:** This tab showcases Apple's own content, available only via your Apple TV+ subscription. Might I suggest *Wolfwalkers* for all ages and *Ted Lasso* for older audiences — both are outstanding!
- **Library:** Browse your library of movies and shows you've purchased through the iTunes Store or the Apple TV app.
- **Search:** Tap the Search button, and then tap a category or the Search field at the top of the window to find your next entertainment choice.

Mac

Figure 4-2 offers a glance at the Apple TV app on macOS.

Watch Now
tv+
Movies
TV Shows
Sports
Library
WOLFWALKERS
Golden Globe® Nominee: Best Animated Feature
Apple Originals: Spring 2021 & Beyond
Watch a special preview of new and upcoming shows and films on Apple TV+.

FIGURE 4-2: The Apple TV app looks a little different for Mac but offers the same goodies.

Select a tab at the top of the window to check out the latest movies and shows from Apple and other providers. You can also buy content through the app.

Other devices and platforms

The Apple TV app can also be found on Apple TV, several smart TVs, popular gaming consoles, most non-Apple streaming devices, and even via your favorite web browser. Figure 4-3 shows you how it looks on an Apple TV device.

Watch Now
Movies
TV Shows
Kids
Library
TED LASSO
Resume Episode
Trent Crimm: The Independent S1, E3: To arrange an in-depth exposé, Rebecca pairs cynical journalist Trent Crimm with Ted for a day. Ted and Roy venture into the community.
Starring Jason Sudeikis, Hannah Waddingham, Juno Temple

FIGURE 4-3: The Apple TV app running on an Apple TV box.

The Apple TV app looks and acts much the same on all other supported devices and platforms. However, you can't access your library through the website. As a matter of fact, the website's functionality is fairly limited and is only supported for Google Chrome or Mozilla Firefox browsers.

Visit the Apple's TV Support site for much more information: `https://support.apple.com/tv`.

IN THIS CHAPTER

» Accessing Apple Arcade on your devices

» Connecting supported controllers

» Finding and downloading games

Chapter 5
Get Your Head in the Game!

I was one of those kids who walked into the local mall and made a beeline for the arcade. Parachute pants or jams sagging from several dollars' worth of quarters in my pockets, I was ready and armed for an afternoon of digital battle. Ah, the glory days of the bright lights, bells and whistles, shouts of victory, and cries of defeat! The mall arcade was even better than shows like *Stranger Things* make them out to be.

Since those times are behind us, Apple's taken the step of bringing the arcade to us. Apple Arcade is a gaming subscription service that's part of Apple One, and it offers complete and unlimited access to over 100 games that you can play on just about any Apple device. You can even begin play on one device and switch to another if batteries are running low or you'd rather take gameplay to a larger screen. There are also no in-game purchases to make, and you can use a supported wireless gaming controller to enhance your experience.

Access Apple Arcade

You must be signed into your Apple ID on the devices you want to use with your Apple Arcade subscription. After you do that, you'll be able to download and play games across a gamut of Apple devices.

REMEMBER

Sorry, Windows and Android users, but Apple Arcade is not supported for either platform. It's also not supported via a website, so there really is no way to access your subscription on those devices.

iPhone and iPad

The App Store is your gateway to blissful hours of Apple Arcade gaming.

First check to see that you're logged into your Apple ID, and then launch the App Store app:

1. **Open the Settings app.**
2. **Ensure that you're logged in to your Apple ID.**

   If you're signed in, you'll see your name at the top of the Settings list. If you don't see your name, tap Sign In to sign in with your Apple ID username and password.
3. **Swipe down the Settings list and tap App Store.**
4. **Several options are available, and I encourage you to peruse them all, but I'm most concerned with the following two:**
   - *Automatic Downloads:* If you want to automatically download apps to your iPhone or iPad that you've already downloaded on your other supported Apple devices, toggle on (green) the switches for Apps and App Updates. This is a good idea if you want to keep the same games on all your devices, but be warned that this setting will apply to all other types of applications as well (if they're supported for multiple Apple products).

     WARNING

     Don't confuse the Automatic Downloads section of the App Store settings page with the Automatic Downloads option in the Cellular Data section on that same page.

- *Cellular Data:* If you want to allow app downloads via your cellular connection when you're not connected to Wi-Fi, toggle on (green) the Automatic Downloads switch.

  TIP

  If you disable the Automatic Downloads option under Cellular Data, you'll be able to download apps only when your device is connected to Wi-Fi, which is what you would prefer if you don't have an unlimited cellular data plan.

5. **Leave the Settings app.**

   If your iPhone or iPad uses Face ID, swipe up to leave the app. If your iPhone or iPad has a Home button, press it to leave Settings.

6. **Tap to open the App Store app.**

Mac

To ensure that you're signed into your Apple Arcade subscription:

1. **Click the App Store icon in the dock to launch the app.**

   The icon looks like a blue circle containing a white *A*. If for some reason you don't see it in the dock, you can find it in your Applications folder.

2. **Click Sign In in the lower-left corner of the App Store window or choose Store ⇨ Sign In from the menu at the top of the screen.**

3. **Type your Apple ID username and password, and then click Sign In.**

   Now you're signed into your Apple Arcade subscription and may begin downloading and playing games on your Mac.

Apple TV

My favorite way of playing Apple Arcade games is through Apple TV (refer to Chapter 4 for more info) due to the larger screen and better sound that I get with the TV and my sound system. The setup is also more like playing games with a gaming console, such as an Xbox or PlayStation (especially when you use a gaming controller), so I just enjoy the experience more.

TIP

When you first set up your Apple TV, you'll be prompted to sign in with your Apple ID. However, if for some reason you've signed out or have multiple Apple IDs, please continue with the following steps.

To make sure you're signed into your Apple Arcade subscription and open the Apple Arcade app:

1. **Click the Settings app on your Apple TV's Home screen using your remote control.**
2. **Select Users and Accounts, and then select Add New User.**
3. **Type your Apple ID username and password, and then click Sign In.**
4. **Press the Menu key on your remote control until you get back to the Home screen, and then click the Arcade app icon.**

   The world of Apple Arcade games opens for you on the big screen.

CONNECT A GAMING CONTROLLER

Although you can use your Apple TV's Siri remote to play many games, most Apple Arcade games let you use a wireless gaming controller — some even require it — which usually offers a much richer in-game experience and affords greater control over the action. The following is a list of supported wireless controllers for Apple Arcade games:

- Xbox Adaptive Controller
- Xbox Elite Wireless Controller Series 2
- Xbox Wireless Controller with Bluetooth (Model 1708)
- PlayStation DualShock 4 Wireless Controller
- Some MFi (made for iOS) Bluetooth controllers

Check out Apple's Support site at `https://support.apple.com/en-us/HT210414` for more information on supported controllers and how to connect them to your devices.

Finding and Downloading Games

You can't play what you don't have, so in this section I describe how to discover and install Apple Arcade games on your Apple devices.

iPhone and iPad

The App Store behaves similarly on iOS and iPadOS. Figure 5-1 shows you the Arcade tab of the App Store.

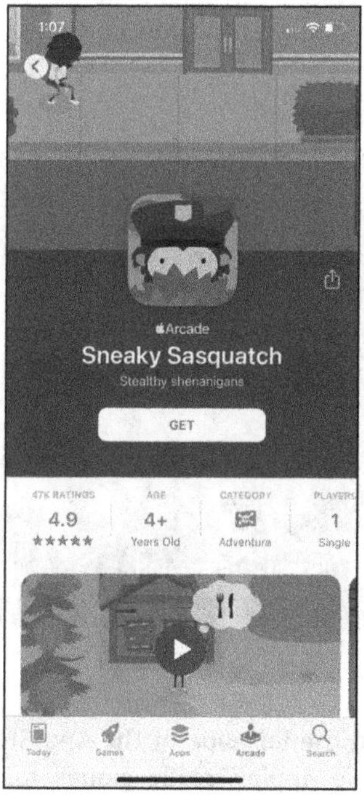
1:07
Arcade
Sneaky Sasquatch
Stealthy shenanigans
GET
4.9
4+
Years Old
Adventure
1
Single
Today
Games
Apps
Arcade
Search

FIGURE 5-1: Checking out a game in the iOS App Store.

Tap the Arcade tab at the bottom of the screen to browse Apple Arcade games that come with your subscription. From here you can:

- **Tap a game title to find out more information about it.** Swipe up and down on the screen to read a description of the game, see reviews by other gamers, and discover other info such as ratings and hardware requirements.
- **Tap the Get button to download and install the game on your iPhone or iPad.**

Mac

Figure 5-2 shows you a game in the Arcade tab of the macOS App Store.

Discover
Arcade
Create
Work
Play
Develop
Categories
Updates
Sneaky Sasquatch
Stealthy shenanigans
GET

FIGURE 5-2: Sneaky Sasquatch is a hugely popular Apple Arcade game.

Select the Arcade tab on the left side of the App Store window and browse the available Apple Arcade games for your Mac. Click a game's title for more information on the game, including reviews, ratings, and controller and other requirements. Click the Get button to download and install the game on your Mac; you'll find it in your Applications folder.

Apple TV

Apple TV has an Arcade app built right in. Simply select it from your Apple TV's Home screen and start checking out the games, as shown in Figure 5-3.

Arcade
Most Popular
Sneaky Sasquatch
Stealthy shenanigans
Sonic Racing
Super Speed Racing
SpongeBob: Patty Pursuit
Save the Krabby Patty Formula
Crossy Road Castle
Endless Co-op Platform Fun
Categories

FIGURE 5-3: The Apple TV app running on an Apple TV box.

Select a game's title for more information, including reviews, ratings, and controller requirements. Select the Get button to download and install the game on your Apple TV, where it will reside on your Home screen.

TIP

You can use folders to organize games and other apps on your Apple TV Home screen, which keep it from getting cluttered. Find out more at `https://support.apple.com/guide/tv/customize-the-home-screen-atvbad14dc6a/tvos`.

3

Lifestyles of the Fit and Informed

IN THIS PART . . .

Catching up on local and world events with Apple News+

Staying on top of your game with Apple Fitness+

IN THIS CHAPTER

» Accessing News+ on your devices

» Find the latest articles and information

» Add, edit, and organize contacts

Chapter 6 Staying Informed with Apple News+

Ah, the news. These days the very word can evoke mixed emotions and angst. But there's much more to the news than negativity; a great deal of positive and truly informative articles are out there for you to read (and listen to). I mention elsewhere my affinity for the old days of grocery store racks of magazines, covering every topic under the sun and just waiting for me to pick up and peruse. As they often do, Apple has taken that concept to the next level.

I give you Apple News+.

Apple News+ (we'll just stick to News+ the rest of the way) is the premium version of Apple News. By default, the News app already brings you the day's latest info to keep you up to date, but a News+ subscription through Apple One opens the pages of hundreds of the world's best newspapers and magazines that journalism has to offer. News, entertainment, sports, food, kids and parenting, women's and men's lifestyles, health, and other topics make sure that there's always something available to read and listen to. You can even read entire digital versions of many print publications right on your iPhone, iPad, and Mac. Some articles also have audio versions, allowing you to listen to them on you iPhone and even in your automobile via CarPlay.

TECHNICAL STUFF

Audio in the News apps is available only for iPhone, iPod touch, and CarPlay and only in the United States.

TIP

Wanna see the list of publications that News+ offers before taking the plunge? Check them out at `www.apple.com/apple-news/publications/`.

News keeps track of the subjects you frequent the most and begins to curate articles most likely to pique your interest. You can also follow publications and get recommendations from Siri. Your preferences follow you from device to device because you must log in to each with your Apple ID to access your News+ subscription.

REMEMBER

To clarify, *News+* is the premium subscription service and *News* is the app used to view your News+ articles. From this point, I refer to *News* when discussing the app and actions you take within it, and *News+* when specifically talking about the subscription plan.

Access News and News+

You need to be signed into your Apple ID on the devices you want to use with your News+ subscription. From there, the News app is your gateway to your own virtual magazine rack.

REMEMBER

The Apple News app is the only way to access your News+ subscription, so I'm afraid there's no way for Windows, Linux, and Android users to take advantage of this great service on their devices. There's no URL or iCloud.com web app for Apple News.

iPhone and iPad

To sync your News+ account with your iOS and iPadOS devices, you must ensure that News is enabled on them.

To enable News synchronization and to open the News app on your iPhone or iPad:

1. **Open the Settings app.**
2. **Tap your Apple ID at the top of the Settings list.**
3. **Tap iCloud.**
4. **Tap the News switch to enable it (if it's not already enabled).**
5. **Leave the Settings app.**

   If your iPhone or iPad uses Face ID, swipe up to leave the Settings app. If your iPhone or iPad has a Home button, press it to leave Settings.
6. **Tap to open the News app.**

   You see the latest news, sports, and other info.

TIP

To keep your News app updated and working its best, be sure that you have the latest version of iOS, iPadOS, or macOS on your devices.

Mac

To get the latest scoop while sitting in front of your desktop or laptop, you need to check that News is enabled on your Mac.

Do the following:

1. **Click the in the top-left corner of your screen and select System Preferences.**
2. **Select Apple ID.**
3. **Select the box next to News to enable it, if it's not already selected.**
4. **Open your Applications folder.**
5. **Double-click the News app icon to open it.**

TIP

You can make sure the News app is always handy by keeping it in your dock. While the News app is open on your Mac, right-click or Control-click its icon in the dock and choose Options⇨Keep in Dock.

All the News That's Fit to Print (or View)

The News app is intelligently designed to work much the same regardless of whether you're using your iPhone, iPad, or Mac. But because two utilize touchscreens and the other is a traditional point-and-click computer with a mouse or trackpad (or both), some bells and whistles may be located in slightly different places.

Perusing the magazine rack

Knowing how to navigate an app is half the battle. After you know where the important things are, you have the freedom to use the app more than learn it.

Usually, iOS and iPadOS versions of an app look and behave a bit more alike than their counterpart on macOS. However, that's not so with News. In this case, the iPadOS and macOS apps are more alike than the iOS iteration, so I follow that convention throughout the rest of the chapter.

iOS

As mentioned, New for iOS works a bit differently than the app for iPadOS and macOS due to its smaller touchscreen interface. There's just not the same amount of screen real estate on an iPhone as there is on a Mac and an iPad.

Figure 6-1 gives you the lowdown for the default News app screen in iOS.

Tap an icon at the bottom of the screen to explore the News app on your iPhone:

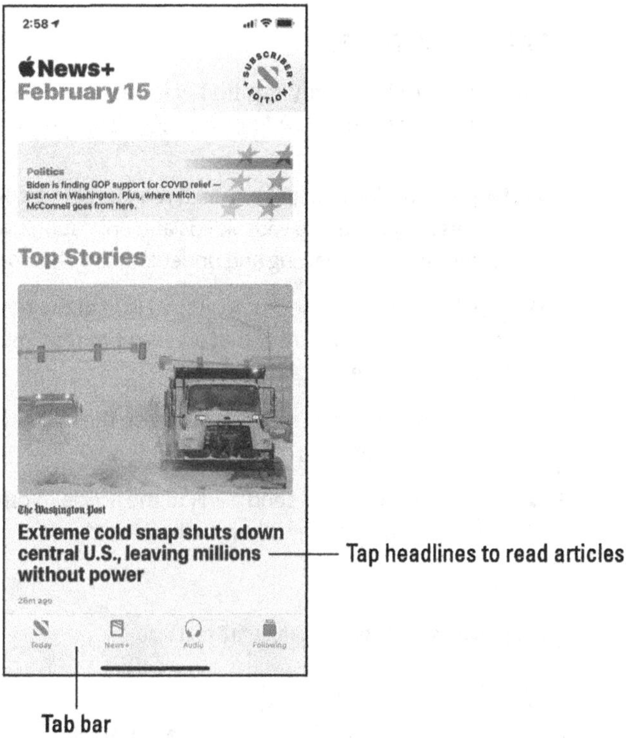
2:58
News+
February 15
Politics
Biden is finding GOP support for COVID relief — just not in Washington. Plus, where Mitch McConnell goes from here.
Top Stories
The Washington Post
Extreme cold snap shuts down central U.S., leaving millions without power
Tap headlines to read articles
Tab bar

FIGURE 6-1: News for iOS is your source for the latest news and best articles.

- **Today:** Tap to see today's top stories as chosen by Apple's editorial staff and based on your preferences. As mentioned, the more you use News the more it learns what subjects tickle your fancy. Swipe down the screen to find articles related to subjects such as sports, politics, and health, see lists and issues recommended for you based on your history, and more. The Today tab is the default when you launch News for the first time in a given day.
- **News+:** Tap to explore the hundreds of magazines and newspapers at your disposal as an Apple One subscriber.

  TIP

  When viewing a magazine or newspaper, swipe left or right to turn the pages.
- **Audio:** Tap to discover articles in audio format, which makes it easier for you to catch up when on the go, whether exercising, riding, driving, or what have you.
- **Following:** Tap to see articles from publications you regularly read, view your reading history, and search for articles.

READING ARTICLES

To read an article, simply tap its headline. Once there, you have a few options, as shown in Figure 6-2:

- Swipe up or down on the article to read its content. Some articles are gussied up with videos and animations, which help immensely in connecting and understanding their message.
- Tap the thumbs-up or thumbs-down icon at the bottom of the screen to let Siri know that you want to read more or less of the same content.
- Tap the AA icon to increase or decrease the text size, which may make it easier to read an article.
- Tap the Share icon to send a link to the article to others via Messages, Mail, or any other method listed.

Go to previous screen
Change the text size
Share this article
Food Network
AA
Dressed-Up Pastas for a Meatless Monday Dinner
by Maria Russo
A guaranteed family favorite, pasta is an easy, economical meal that feeds a crowd. Tonight, instead of resorting to traditional spaghetti with simple tomato sauce, try experimenting with oddly shaped noodles, such as orecchiette, and new, cre-
Rate this article
Go to previous or next article

FIGURE 6-2: Use these icons to navigate an article.

LISTENING TO ARTICLES

If an article has an audio version, you'll see a Listen label at the top of it (see Figure 6-3, left) or a headphone icon next to its headline (or both). When the article is playing you'll see its title at the bottom of the screen. Tap the title to view the playback controls for the article (see Figure 6-3, right) and swipe down from the top of the screen to close the player.

Tap to listen
Swipe down to close player
5:11
VANITY FAIR
AA
Listen 36 min left
The Wanderer
PETER BEARD'S legacy as artist and flaneur is a rich one, but even in death, shadows loom
By STACEY STOWE
Open
NOVEMBER 2020
1:10
VANITY FAIR
The Last Days of a Real-Life Indiana
00:40
-36:06
15
1x
Playback speed
Play/pause
Volume slider
Drag playhead to move back and forth

FIGURE 6-3: Tap Listen to hear an audio article and control its playback.

FOLLOWING PUBLICATIONS

The Following tab allows you to search for articles and publications, as well as follow your favorites. To follow publications:

1. **At the bottom of the main News app screen, tap the Following icon.**
2. **Swipe down and tap Discover Channels & Topics.**
3. **Tap publications to select (follow) or deselect (unfollow) them, as shown in Figure 6-4.**
4. **Tap Done when you're finished.**

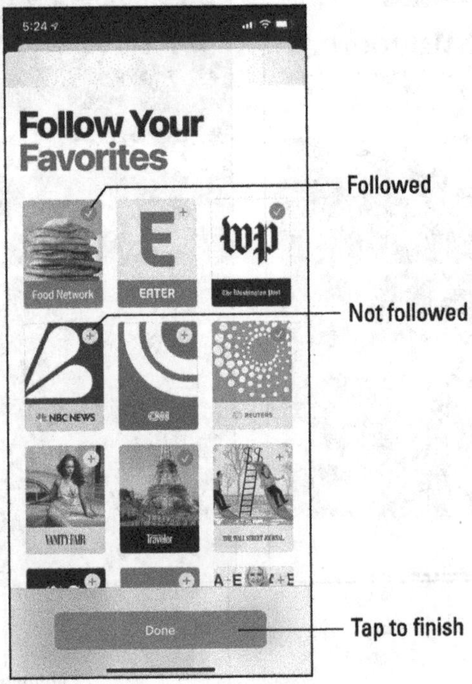
5:24
Follow Your Favorites
Followed
Food Network
EATER
Not followed
NBC NEWS
CNN
REUTERS
VANITY FAIR
Traveler
THE WALL STREET JOURNAL.
A+E
Done
Tap to finish

FIGURE 6-4: Tap publication icons to follow or unfollow them.

macOS and iPadOS

News for macOS and iPadOS function much the same; in this section you take a gander at getting around in News so you can get caught up on today's latest.

TIP

Many News features in macOS and iPadOS are similar to those in News for iOS and have been discussed in the previous sections. You may want to refer to those sections for more information if you don't find it in the following.

Figure 6-5 is your News for macOS and iPadOS quick start guide.

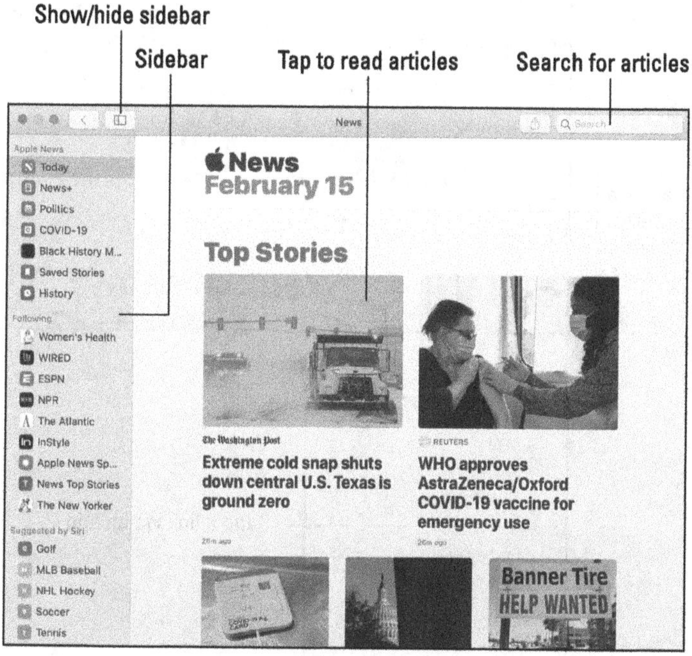
Show/hide sidebar
Sidebar
Tap to read articles
Search for articles
News
Apple News
Today
News+
Politics
COVID-19
Black History M...
Saved Stories
History
Following
Women's Health
WIRED
ESPN
NPR
The Atlantic
InStyle
Apple News Sp...
News Top Stories
The New Yorker
Suggested by Siri
Golf
MLB Baseball
NHL Hockey
Soccer
Tennis
News
February 15
Top Stories
The Washington Post
Extreme cold snap shuts down central U.S. Texas is ground zero
REUTERS
WHO approves AstraZeneca/Oxford COVID-19 vaccine for emergency use
Banner Tire
HELP WANTED

FIGURE 6-5: News works basically the same for macOS and iPadOS.

Click an article's headline to read it. Figure 6-6 shows an open article and lists a couple of important features.

The Share icon (labeled in Figure 6-6) in News for macOS and iPadOS affords several options you find in other locations in News for iOS. Figure 6-7 spells those out for you.

This chapter has given you the scoop on News for your Apple devices and how to take advantage of your News+ subscription. For more info, check out Apple's Support site for News at `https://support.apple.com/en-us/HT202329`.

Previous screen
Share icon
News
Apple News
Today
News+
Politics
COVID-19
Black History M...
Saved Stories
History
Following
Food Network
The Washingto...
Condé Nast Tra...
Reuters
National Geogr...
Women's Health
WIRED
ESPN
NPR
The Atlantic
InStyle
Apple News Sp...
News Top Stories
The New Yorker
Suggested by Siri
SWIPE TO SEE MORE
TAP IMAGES ABOVE FOR CAPTIONS
Want dreamy

FIGURE 6-6: Reading an article in News for macOS and iPadOS.

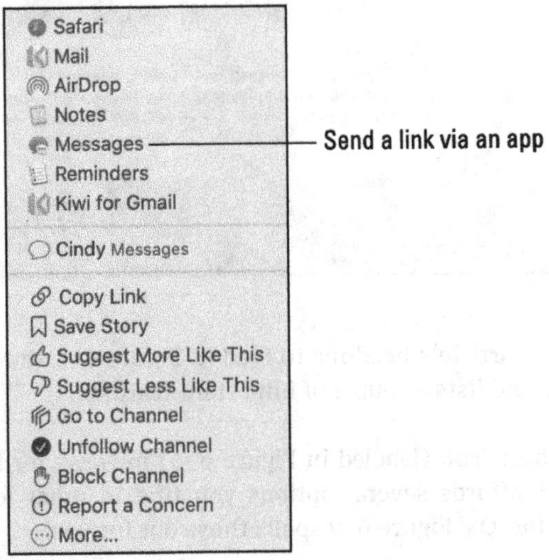
Safari
Mail
AirDrop
Notes
Messages
Reminders
Kiwi for Gmail
Cindy Messages
Copy Link
Save Story
Suggest More Like This
Suggest Less Like This
Go to Channel
Unfollow Channel
Block Channel
Report a Concern
More...
Send a link via an app

FIGURE 6-7: The Share button in News for macOS and iPadOS is full of options.

» Discovering workout types and trainers

» Tracking your metrics and progress

Chapter 7
Fitness Fanatics +

Keeping in shape is tough. I write that as I sit next to a warm box of Dunkin' Munchkins, with the delicious little devils tempting me with their sweet aroma. I'll try to ignore them as I write this chapter.

Digital devices can either hinder or help us as we strive to stay on top of our health. Although they offer such sedentary activities as browsing social media, playing games, and checking the daily news and email, they can also help us set and meet our fitness goals.

Apple's latest addition to its services lineup is Apple Fitness+. A Fitness+ subscription opens the door to workouts of all types led by some of the best personal trainers in the fitness world. Using the Apple Watch, Fitness+ can also help you monitor your body's vital statistics while you work out, offering a new level of health tracking. Fitness+ also helps curate your workouts based on your previous exercise activities.

REMEMBER

You must have an Apple Watch to sign up for Fitness+. You don't always need to be wearing it to work out, however.

Access Fitness+

You must be signed into your Apple ID on the devices you want to use with your Fitness+ subscription. You'll then be able to exercise and monitor your workout from just about anywhere.

Supported devices

Fitness+ is an Apple-only service, meaning you can't access it on any non-Apple devices, period. You also can't access it with your Mac. So what the heck can you access it with? Fitness+ requires an Apple Watch Series 3 or newer to sign up and supports the following devices for finding and starting workouts:

- **iPhone 6s or newer running iOS 14.3 or newer**
- **iPad running iPadOS 14.3 or newer**
- **Apple TV running tvOS 14.3 or newer**

iPhone and iPad

The Fitness app may come installed with iOS on your iPhone. If not, you can also download it from the App Store on your iPhone and iPad.

TIP

If you have an iPad and haven't downloaded the Fitness app, go ahead and do so before continuing.

Next, check to see that you're logged into your Apple ID, look to see if you're syncing Health settings, and then launch the Fitness app:

1. **Open the Settings app.**
2. **Ensure that you're logged in to your Apple ID.**

   If you're signed in, you'll see your name at the top of the Settings list. If you don't see your name, tap Sign In to sign in with your Apple ID username and password.
3. **Tap your name at the top of the Settings list, and then tap iCloud.**

4. **If you want to sync your workout data with iCloud, toggle on (green) the Health switch.**

   Syncing just makes your workout data available to the Health app on all your Apple devices. You don't have to do this, but if you don't, your health statistics may differ from device to device.

5. **Leave the Settings app.**

   If your iPhone or iPad uses Face ID, swipe up to leave the app. If your iPhone or iPad has a Home button, press it to leave Settings.

6. **Tap to open the Fitness app.**

Apple TV

The Fitness app on your iPhone or iPad is the obvious way to go if you're working outside or away from home. But if you are home, I think that the Fitness app on Apple TV wins the day.

To make sure you're signed into your Fitness+ subscription and open the Fitness app, do the following:

1. **Click the Settings app on your Apple TV's Home screen using your remote control.**
2. **Select Users and Accounts, and then select Add New User.**
3. **Type your Apple ID username and password, and then click Sign In.**
4. **Press the Menu key on your remote control until you get back to the Home screen, and then click the Fitness app icon.**

Finding and Starting Workouts

Fitness+ has a great lineup of trainers who are able to help anyone at any fitness level achieve their goals. You select the type of workout you want, choose a trainer and length of training time, and then select the type of music you'd like to use. It doesn't get much simpler.

REMEMBER

Before we go any further, be sure to strap on your Apple Watch if you want to save workout data and track your progress during the workout.

Finding a workout

The Fitness app for iPhone and iPad displays a Fitness+ tab at the bottom of the screen if you own an Apple Watch. Tap the Fitness+ tab to get rolling.

For Apple TV, launch the Fitness app and select the name of your Apple Watch, or select Other if your Apple Watch isn't paired with your Apple TV.

TIP

To pair your Apple Watch with your Apple TV, just enter the code displayed on your Apple TV in the Workout app of your Apple Watch when prompted.

(Do you hear that? Those Munchkins are calling my name . . . must resist!)

After you're in the app, it's time to find a workout:

1. **Select a workout type from the list, as shown at the bottom of Figure 7-1.**

   You can choose from HIIT (high intensity interval training), Yoga, Core, Strength, Treadmill (Walk or Run), Cycling, Rowing, Dance, and Mindful Cooldown.

2. **Tap or click the Filter button.**
3. **Choose a trainer from the list, as shown in Figure 7-2.**
4. **Select a time interval for your session.**
5. **Decide the type of music you'd like to use during your workout.**
6. **Select a workout from the filtered list (seen in Figure 7-3) to preview or see a list of music related to it.**

   If you're on an iPhone or iPad, you can tap the + Add button to save the workout to My Workouts at the bottom of the Fitness+ screen.

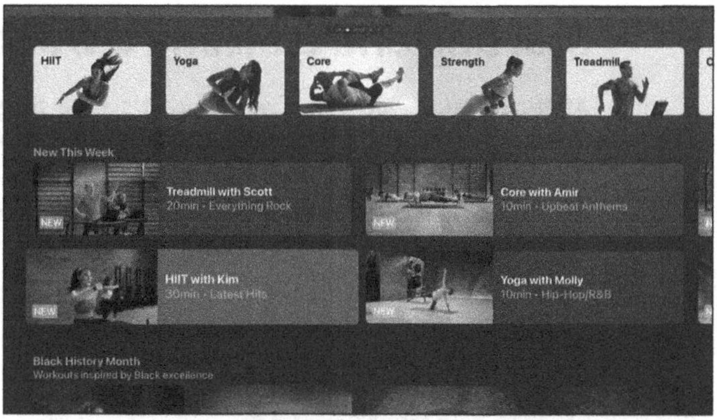
HIIT
Yoga
Core
Strength
Treadmill
New This Week
Treadmill with Scott
20min · Everything Rock
NEW
Core with Amir
10min · Upbeat Anthems
HIIT with Kim
30min · Latest Hits
NEW
Yoga with Molly
10min · Hip-Hop/R&B
NEW
Black History Month
Workouts inspired by Black excellence

FIGURE 7-1: Choose a workout type to begin.

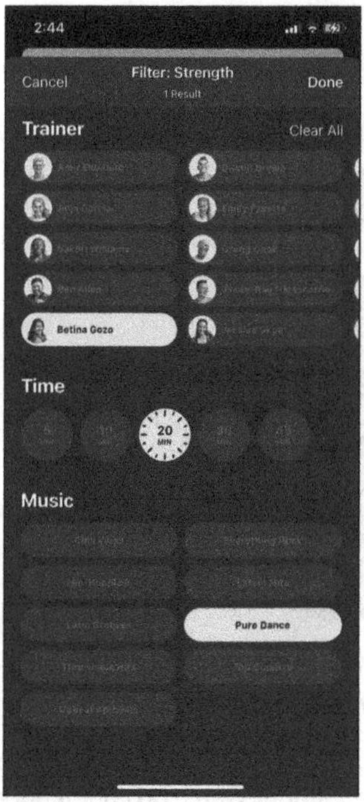
2:44
Cancel
Filter: Strength
1 Result
Done
Trainer
Clear All
Betina Gozo
Time
20 MIN
Music
Pure Dance

FIGURE 7-2: The Trainer, Time, and Music filters help you whittle down your selections.

Fitness+
Strength
Filter
Increase total-body fitness and make everyday moves like bending, twisting, and lifting easier with the functional strength exercises in Fitness+ Strength. Dynamic sequences target upp... more
Workouts
Sort
Pure Dance
Betina Gozo
20MIN
Strength with Betina
20min · Pure Dance

FIGURE 7-3: I've successfully narrowed my workout choices.

Starting and tracking a workout

After you've decided on a workout, it's time to get moving! To start your workout in Fitness for iOS, iPadOS, or Apple TV:

1. **Tap or select the Let's Go button when viewing the workout information, as shown in Figure 7-4.**

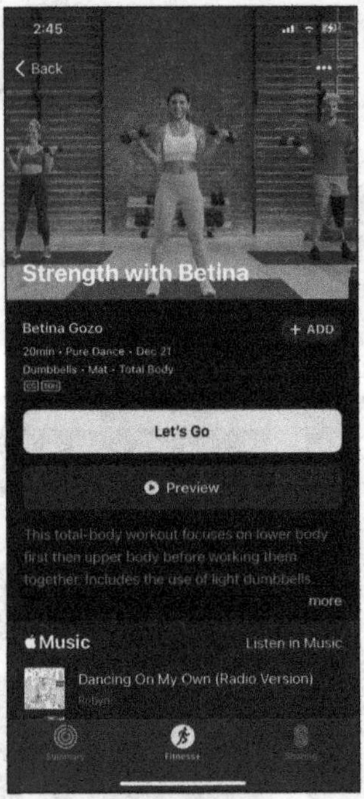

2:45
Back
Strength with Betina
Betina Gozo
+ ADD
20min · Pure Dance · Dec 21
Dumbbells · Mat · Total Body
Let's Go
Preview
This total-body workout focuses on lower body first then upper body before working them together. Includes the use of light dumbbells.
more
Music
Listen in Music
Dancing On My Own (Radio Version)

FIGURE 7-4: Tap Let's Go to launch your workout.

2. **Tap or select the brightly colored play icon to get going.**

   If you don't have your Apple Watch handy or don't want to wear it, tap Work Out without Watch on your iPhone or iPad screen.

3. **Pause and continue your workout as you like using the touchscreen on your iPhone, iPad, or Apple Watch, or with your Apple TV's remote control.**

   As you work out, your metrics and stats are displayed on your iPhone, iPad, or television screen.

4. **When you're finished, check out your workout metrics and stats, which are displayed on your device's screen.**

TIP

What kind of equipment might you need to use with Fitness+? That depends on the type of workout you'd like to do. For example, you can't very well take part in a cycling workout if you don't have access to a bicycle. You can use just about any kind of exercise equipment you prefer, but if you'd like to see a list of products Apple recommends, visit www.apple.com/apple-fitness-plus/equipment.

4 Every iCloud Has a Silver Lining

IN THIS PART . . .

Getting a handle on iCloud

Storing your files online with iCloud Drive

Saving and sharing photos and videos in iCloud Photos

Sending and receiving email in iCloud Mail

Creating and syncing calendars and reminders

Authoring notes and managing contacts

Staying productive in the cloud with Pages, Numbers, and Keynote

Finding lost devices and looking up friends

it works

» Determining how much storage you'll need

» Getting to iCloud from all your devices

Chapter 8
Walking on iCloud Nine

Have some great photos you'd like to share with the world right this instant?

Do you wish you could work on the chapter of that book while on your train ride into the city, but it's on your iPad at work?

Wouldn't it stink if you were cooking dinner at a friend's house, only to realize you left the recipe on your computer at home?

Remember just how unpleasant it was the last time your computer crashed and you lost everything you had on it?

Or how about the ultimate fright for an Apple fan — have you ever lost your iPhone and had no idea where it could be hiding?

Sorry to raise your blood pressure at the mere thought of some of those scenarios. No worries, though, dear reader: Apple has your back with a nifty service called iCloud. Let's jump right in and find out what iCloud is all about and how it can make your life so much easier.

What Is iCloud?

iCloud helps you keep your stuff safe, secure, synchronized, and accessible from any Internet-capable device anywhere in the world. How's that for a succinct definition? And it's not an exaggeration.

The word *iCloud* comes from the term *cloud computing,* with Apple's signature *i* tacked onto the front. Cloud computing uses the Internet (a.k.a. the *cloud*) to provide services, such as storage and applications, you'd normally be able to get only from your computer's built-in hardware.

For example, you know how to store files, such as text documents and PDFs, in a folder on your computer. As great as that is, you're limited to accessing those files from that specific computer. Now, with cloud computing, you can store those files in the cloud and access them from any device anywhere on the planet as long the device can connect to the Internet.

iCloud is Apple's version of cloud computing, so rest assured that its user-friendliness and reliability are world-class. It's also much more than just a place to store files. iCloud includes applications that help you share photos and videos, keep track of your daily schedule, communicate with the world, be productive, and even find that lost iPhone I mentioned earlier. Here's a rundown of some of iCloud's more popular perks:

- **iCloud Drive** is a virtual hard drive where you can store just about any content. Music, spreadsheets, videos, archived files — iCloud Drive supports just about any kind of file in the cloud. Chapter 9 discusses iCloud Drive in greater detail.
- **iCloud Photos** stores and synchronizes your photos and videos across your devices. You can upload photos and videos automatically or manually, and share them with ridiculous simplicity. You find out more in Chapter 10.
- **Mail** is an email service that you can access with any email client or any Internet browser. Chapter 11 helps you get started.
- **Calendar** keeps your appointments in the cloud and available on every device. You can add, edit, and delete

events from any Internet-connected computer, smartphone, or tablet. Discover more in Chapter 12.

- **Reminders** helps you keep track of your to-do lists. See Chapter 12 for this topic, too.
- **Notes** gives you a place to create simple text documents, scan paper documents, and even scribble handwritten notes. Chapter 13 gets you up-to-speed quickly.
- **Contacts** keeps your contact information in one convenient place so that all contacts are accessible from any Internet-ready device. See Chapter 13 for more on this subject.
- **Pages, Numbers, and Keynote** are Apple's word processor, spreadsheet application, and presentation software, respectively. Use them to be productive anywhere, whether on your iPhone, iPad, Mac, or any other device that connects to the Internet. Chapter 14 will help you get going with all three apps.
- **Find My** helps you locate devices and people, as long as they're connected to the Internet via Wi-Fi or cellular. Check out Chapter 15 for more information.

iCloud ON WINDOWS? CERTAINLY!

Yes, indeed, you can use iCloud with Windows, and even sync some of the information from your PC with your Apple devices. If this sounds like some sort of dark magic, it very well may be, but nevertheless it works!

The iCloud for Windows app is simple to set up and can be used to sync your PC's photos, email and contacts from Outlook, bookmarks from Internet Explorer or Edge, and more. You can even use the app to create, access, and share files stored on your iCloud Drive.

iCloud for Windows supports Windows 7, 8, and 10. Visit Apple's Support site at `https://support.apple.com/en-hk/HT204283` to download the app, and be sure to click the other links on the page to find out how to best use the various features it offers.

Aside from the ability to access any document or file from anywhere, my favorite feature of iCloud is that any changes you make on one device are automatically synchronized and reflected on your other devices. Let's say you work on a document on your iPhone while in your dentist's waiting room, and then open the same document later on your Mac at home. Any changes you made while waiting for your yearly cleaning will be ready and waiting when you and your pearly whites get back home.

REMEMBER

You must be signed in to the same iCloud account on each of your devices for syncing to work across them. Find out how to sign in to iCloud on your devices later in this chapter.

The Storage Conundrum

iCloud will store your stuff for you, but only you can decide just how much storage space you'll need. Unfortunately, no one-size-fits-all answer exists for this one; it depends entirely on your individual needs.

Anyone who signs up for iCloud (by setting up an Apple ID, for example) gets 5GB of storage free. That's rarely enough for most folks, especially if they plan on using iCloud to back up their devices. Signing up for an Apple One plan will quickly resolve that issue:

- **Individual plan:** Offers 50GB of storage, plus Apple Music, AppleTV+, and Apple Arcade, for $14.95 per month.
- **Family plan:** Boosts your storage to a hefty 200GB and comes with Apple Music, AppleTV+, and Apple Arcade for $19.95 per month.
- **Premier plan:** Lives up to its lofty name by providing a whopping 2TB of storage — that's ten times as much as the Family plan! It also tosses in News+ and Fitness+ for good measure (along with Apple Music, AppleTV+, and Apple Arcade) for $29.95 per month.

What if you want the Individual or Family plan, but still need more than the respective 50GB and 200GB storage amounts? Or what if you have the Premier plan but need even more than 2TB? No problem. Apple enables you to purchase additional storage:

» An additional 50GB costs a cool $0.99 a month.

» An extra 200GB runs you $2.99 a month.

» Go big with an extra 2TB for $9.99 per month.

TIP

The additional storage is supplemental to the storage amount of your plan. For example, if you have the Apple One Family plan, which includes 200GB, purchasing another 50GB will bump your storage up to 250GB. You can max out your storage capacity at a staggering 4TB by going with the Premier plan and adding 2TB.

Visit `https://support.apple.com/en-us/HT201238` for more information on upgrading your iCloud storage.

Signing In and Accessing iCloud

Again, to hammer the point, the true beauty of iCloud is that you can get to all your digital goodies from just about any Internet-connected device in the world. First, let me show you how to sign in to iCloud on your Apple devices, and then I'll tell you how to access those files from just about anywhere.

Signing in to iCloud

You must be signed in to your iCloud account to access and sync your files across devices. You can also enable or disable features and apps to control what you're syncing to the cloud.

To sign in to iCloud on your Mac, follow these simple steps:

1. **Open System Preferences.**

   To do so, click the icon in the upper-left corner of the screen and select System Preferences from the menu.

2. **Click Internet Accounts.**
3. **Select the iCloud option.**
4. **Enter the Apple ID for the iCloud account you're logging into, as shown in Figure 8-1, and then click Next.**

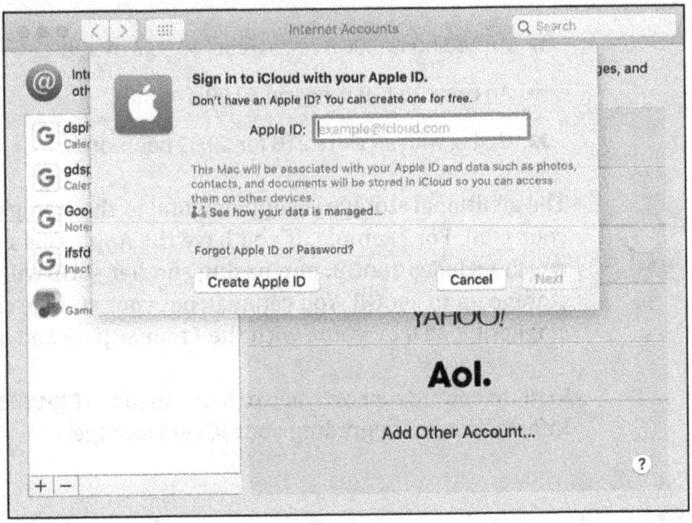
Internet Accounts
Search
Sign in to iCloud with your Apple ID.
Don't have an Apple ID? You can create one for free.
Apple ID:
example@icloud.com
This Mac will be associated with your Apple ID and data such as photos, contacts, and documents will be stored in iCloud so you can access them on other devices.
See how your data is managed...
Forgot Apple ID or Password?
Create Apple ID
Cancel
Next
YAHOO!
Aol.
Add Other Account...

FIGURE 8-1: Log into your account here.

5. **Enter the password for the Apple ID and click Next.**

   Your iCloud account appears on the left side of the Internet Accounts window. The right side of the window displays various features and apps that can be synced with iCloud, as shown in Figure 8-2.

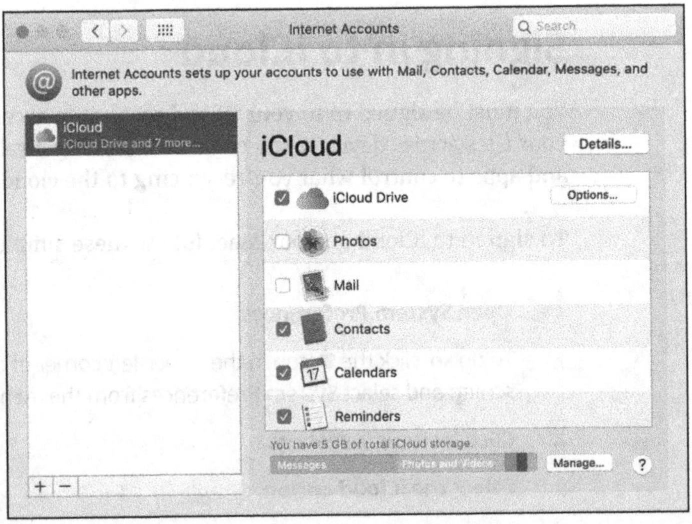
Internet Accounts
Search
Internet Accounts sets up your accounts to use with Mail, Contacts, Calendar, Messages, and other apps.
iCloud
iCloud Drive and 7 more...
iCloud
Details...
iCloud Drive
Options...
Photos
Mail
Contacts
Calendars
Reminders
You have 5 GB of total iCloud storage.
Manage...

FIGURE 8-2: Features and apps are on the right.

6. **Select the boxes next to the features and apps you want to use with your iCloud account.**

To sign in to iCloud on your iPhone or iPad:

1. **Tap the Settings app.**
2. **Tap Sign In to Your iPhone or Sign In to Your iPad.**
3. **Enter the Apple ID for the iCloud account you're logging into, and then click Next in the upper-right corner (see Figure 8-3).**
4. **Enter the password for the Apple ID and tap Next.**

   The Apple ID screen appears (sometimes after a few seconds).
5. **Tap iCloud.**
6. **Tap to toggle the switch next to each item you'd like to enable or disable, as illustrated in Figure 8-4.**

   An item or feature is enabled when the switch is green.

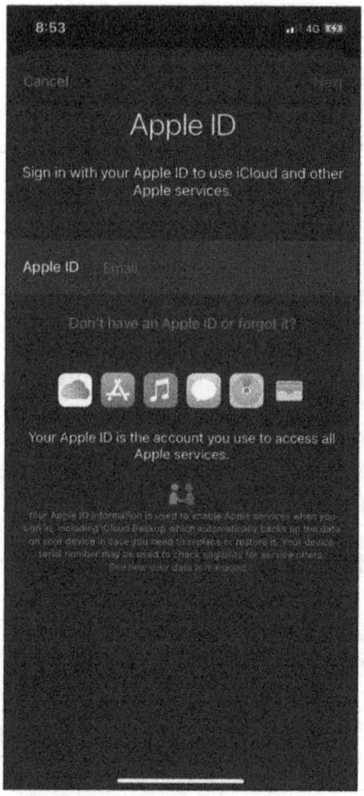
8:53
Cancel
Apple ID
Sign in with your Apple ID to use iCloud and other Apple services.
Apple ID
Don't have an Apple ID or forgot it?
Your Apple ID is the account you use to access all Apple services.

FIGURE 8-3: Enter your Apple ID.

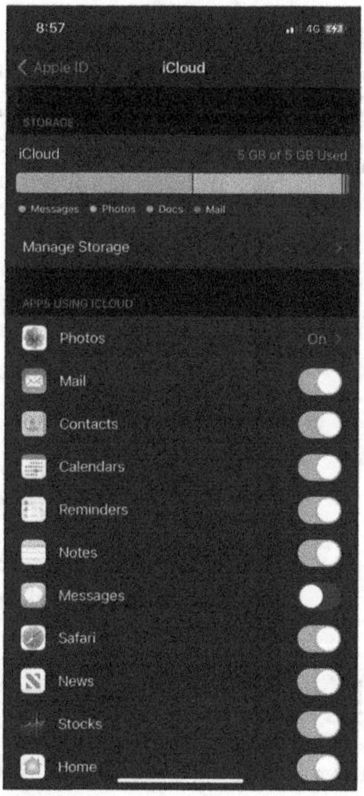
8:57
Apple ID
iCloud
STORAGE
iCloud
5 GB of 5 GB Used
Messages
Photos
Docs
Mail
Manage Storage
APPS USING ICLOUD
Photos
On
Mail
Contacts
Calendars
Reminders
Notes
Messages
Safari
News
Stocks
Home

FIGURE 8-4: Tap to toggle switches for items you want to enable.

Accessing iCloud

Your Mac, iPhone, and iPad come loaded with apps that are built to work seamlessly with iCloud. A few examples are iCloud Drive, Mail, Calendar, Contacts, Notes, Pages, Keynote, Numbers, Safari, Photos, Reminders, and News.

Opening these apps on your Mac, iPhone, or iPad will allow you to access and work with your files, events, reminders, or whathave-you, as long as you're signed in to your iCloud account.

But, what if you're using a device that isn't signed in to your iCloud account? Perhaps you're using a friend's tablet or a computer in an office on the other side of the world. How do you access your iCloud content then? iCloud.com is your answer. You can access iCloud.com from most web browsers on most devices, but some features may not be available in the web-only version of iCloud.

TECHNICAL STUFF

Supported browsers include Safari, Firefox, Google Chrome, Microsoft Edge, Opera, and Internet Explorer. Some functionality may be limited if you're using Android or Linux devices. I advise that you check out the system requirements for iCloud at `https://support.apple.com/en-us/HT204230` for more detailed information.

To sign in to iCloud through a web browser:

1. **Open a supported web browser on a computer, tablet, or smartphone.**
2. **Enter your Apple ID and click the arrow to the right, as shown in Figure 8-5.**
3. **Enter the password for your Apple ID and click the arrow to the right.**

   WARNING

   I don't recommend selecting the Keep Me Signed In box if you're on a computer or device that isn't yours. This will make your iCloud information available to other users of the computer, which is an especially bad idea if the computer is in a public setting, such as a library.
4. **Click one of the icons shown in Figure 8-6 to access the corresponding iCloud feature or app.**

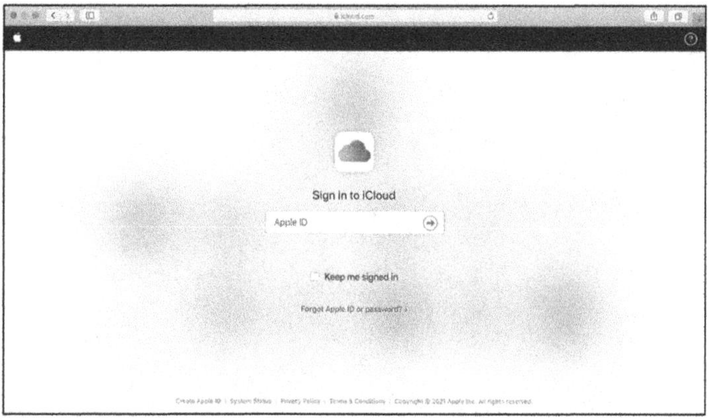
Sign in to iCloud
Apple ID
Keep me signed in
Forgot Apple ID or password?

FIGURE 8-5: Enter your Apple ID and click the arrow.

Monday
4
Mail
Contacts
Calendar
Photos
iCloud Drive
Notes
Reminders
Pages
Numbers
Keynote
Find Friends
Find iPhone

FIGURE 8-6: Apps available in iCloud.com.

Now that you have a better understanding of iCloud, let's dive in a bit deeper and find out how you can make good use of this handy-dandy tool.

IN THIS CHAPTER

- » Enabling iCloud Drive on your devices
- » Understanding supported file types
- » Managing files and folders

Chapter 9
Buckle Up and Drive!

If you've ever used a computer before, you're used to saving your files on drives of some sort: internal or external hard drives or perhaps a USB flash drive. These drives act like filing cabinets, allowing you to organize and store your important documents in one easy-to-access place. iCloud Drive is the cloud-based equivalent of those drives, but with one huge difference: You can get to iCloud Drive on any computer, smartphone, or tablet from anywhere you have Internet access. That sure beats lugging a file cabinet around everywhere, doesn't it?

Read on to discover how to access and utilize iCloud Drive to sync and store your files in one convenient location accessible to all your devices.

Accessing iCloud Drive on Your Devices

iCloud Drive is available as an app for your iPhone, iPad, Mac, and Windows-based PC. You can also access your iCloud Drive from anywhere by using a web browser on any Internet-connected device.

TIP

Before you proceed, make sure you're running the latest version of your device's operating system. iPhones run iOS, iPads use iPadOS (fitting, huh?), Macs go with macOS (seeing a pattern here?), and most PCs run Windows.

iPhone and iPad

iCloud Drive is accessed via the Files app, which is part of iOS for iPhones and iPadOS for iPads.

TECHNICAL STUFF

The Files app can access your stuff on more than just iCloud Drive. You can use it to store files directly on your iPhone or iPad. You can use it also with other cloud-based services, such as Dropbox and Google Drive. For more information, check out this article on Apple's Support site: `https://support.apple.com/en-us/HT206481`.

To use Files with iCloud Drive, first make sure you have iCloud Drive enabled on your iPhone or iPad:

1. **Open the Settings app and tap your Apple ID at the top of the screen.**
2. **Tap the iCloud option.**
3. **Scroll through the list of features until you see iCloud Drive, and then toggle its switch to on (green), as shown in Figure 9-1.**

Next, to access iCloud Drive from your iPhone or iPad, do the following:

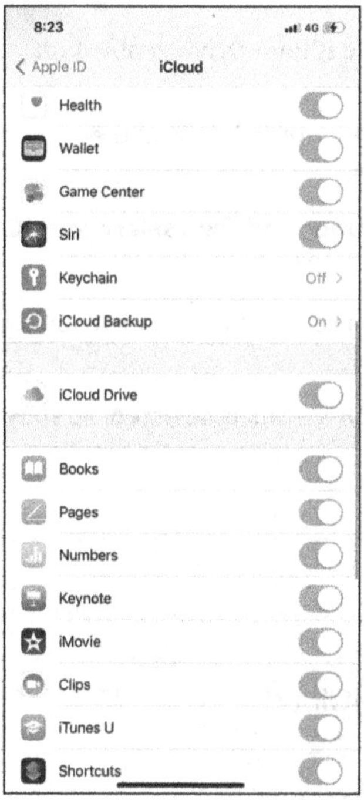
8:23
4G
Apple ID
iCloud
Health
Wallet
Game Center
Siri
Keychain
Off
iCloud Backup
On
iCloud Drive
Books
Pages
Numbers
Keynote
iMovie
Clips
iTunes U
Shortcuts

FIGURE 9-1: Toggle the iCloud Drive switch to on.

1. **Open the Files app.**
2. **If you're not already on the Browse screen, tap the Browse button at the bottom of the screen.**
3. **Tap iCloud Drive under the Locations heading.**

   You see all your content.

Mac

The latest versions of macOS come with iCloud Drive as part of Finder, which is the foundational user interface for your Mac. If you're wondering how to get to Finder, just click the smiley face icon in the dock (as shown in Figure 9-2).

Finder

FIGURE 9-2: Finder is always happy to see you.

Let's make sure you have iCloud Drive enabled on your Mac:

1. **Click the icon in the upper left, and then select System Preferences.**
2. **Click Internet Accounts, and then select your iCloud account.**

   If you've not signed in yet, refer to Chapter 8 for help doing so.
3. **Be sure the iCloud Drive box is selected, as shown in Figure 9-3.**

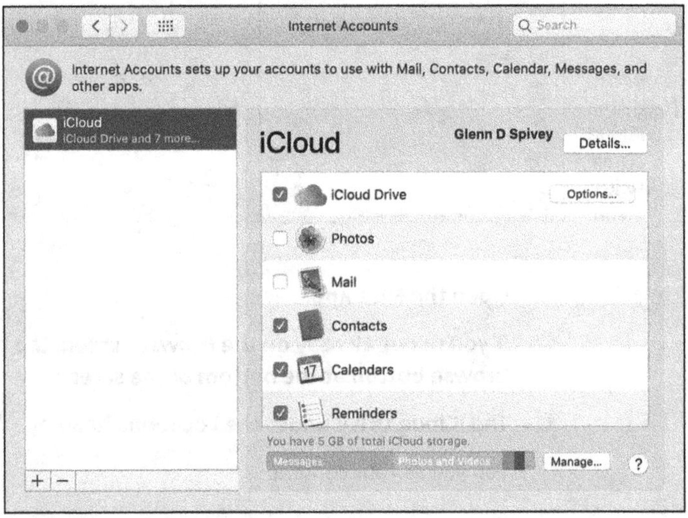

Internet Accounts
Search
Internet Accounts sets up your accounts to use with Mail, Contacts, Calendar, Messages, and other apps.
iCloud
iCloud Drive and 7 more...
iCloud
Glenn D Spivey
Details...
iCloud Drive
Options...
Photos
Mail
Contacts
Calendars
Reminders
You have 5 GB of total iCloud storage.
Manage...

FIGURE 9-3: Select the box next to iCloud Drive to enable it on your Mac.

To access iCloud Drive on your Mac:

1. **Open a Finder window by clicking the Finder icon in the dock.**
2. **At the top of the screen, choose File ⇨ New Finder Window.**
3. **On the left side of the Finder window, click iCloud Drive.**

   You see your files and folders, as shown in Figure 9-4.

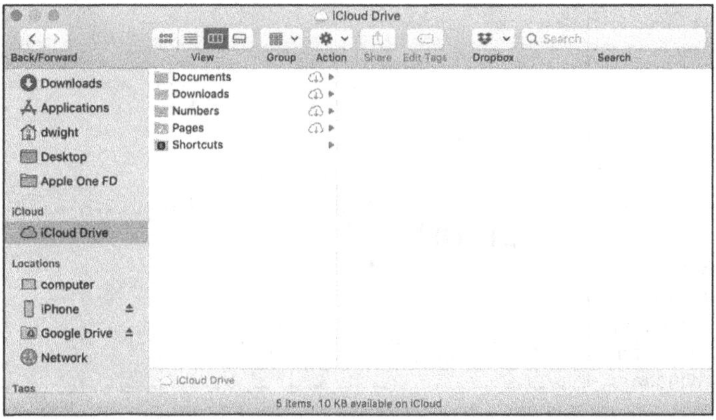
iCloud Drive
Back/Forward
View
Group
Action
Share
Edit Tags
Dropbox
Search
Downloads
Applications
dwight
Desktop
Apple One FD
iCloud
iCloud Drive
Locations
computer
iPhone
Google Drive
Network
Tags
Documents
Downloads
Numbers
Pages
Shortcuts
iCloud Drive
5 items, 10 KB available on iCloud

FIGURE 9-4: iCloud Drive is in Finder's sidebar.

Windows-based PC

iCloud Drive is available as an app for Windows 10. You can download it from the Microsoft Store. For more information, visit the Download iCloud for Windows article on Apple's Support site: `https://support.apple.com/en-us/HT204283`.

TIP

Be sure to set up your iCloud account on your Apple devices before you set it up on your PC. Things will work more smoothly that way, according to Apple.

After you've downloaded the iCloud for Windows app, do the following:

1. **Open the iCloud app.**
2. **Enter your Apple ID and password in the appropriate fields, as shown in Figure 9-5.**
3. **Click the Sign In button in the lower-right corner.**
4. **Make sure the iCloud Drive check box is selected, and then click the Apply button in the lower right.**
5. **To access iCloud Drive, click it in the left pane in the File Explorer window, as shown in Figure 9-6.**

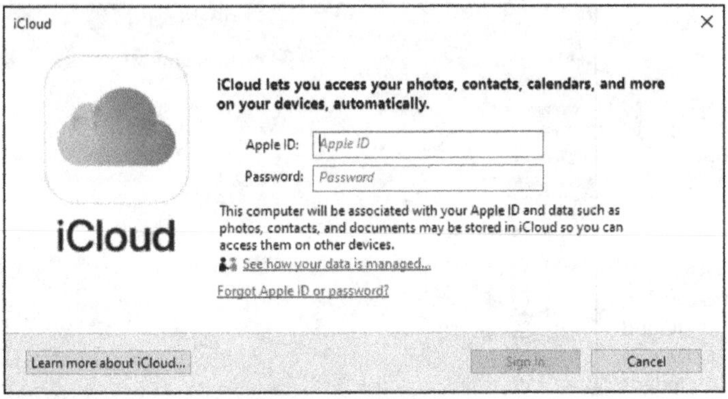
iCloud
iCloud lets you access your photos, contacts, calendars, and more on your devices, automatically.
Apple ID:
Apple ID
Password:
Password
This computer will be associated with your Apple ID and data such as photos, contacts, and documents may be stored in iCloud so you can access them on other devices.
See how your data is managed...
Forgot Apple ID or password?
iCloud
Learn more about iCloud...
Sign In
Cancel

FIGURE 9-5: Logging in to iCloud Drive for Windows.

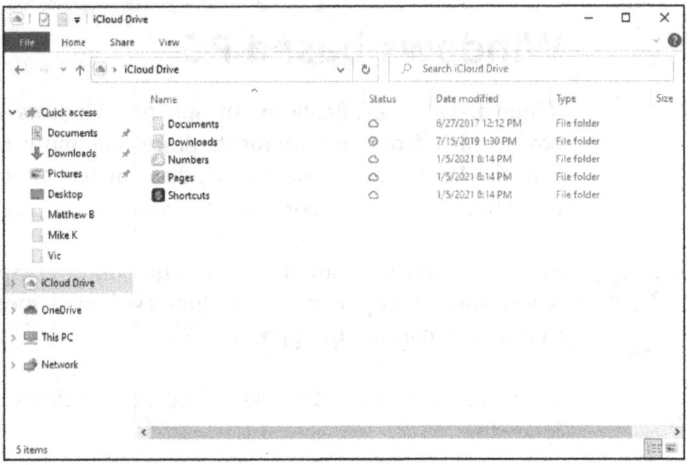
iCloud Drive
File
Home
Share
View
iCloud Drive
Search iCloud Drive
Name
Status
Date modified
Type
Size
Quick access
Documents
Downloads
Pictures
Desktop
Matthew B
Mike K
Vic
iCloud Drive
OneDrive
This PC
Network
Documents
Downloads
Numbers
Pages
Shortcuts
6/27/2017 12:12 PM
7/15/2019 1:30 PM
1/5/2021 8:14 PM
1/5/2021 8:14 PM
1/5/2021 8:14 PM
File folder
File folder
File folder
File folder
File folder
5 items

FIGURE 9-6: Find iCloud Drive in File Explorer's left sidebar.

iCloud.com

You can also get to your iCloud Drive from just about any web browser on an Internet-connected computer, smartphone, or tablet. Be sure that you're using the latest version of the web browser. Safari, Google Chrome, Firefox, Microsoft Edge, Brave, Opera, and other browsers should work just fine.

TIP

If you're using an Android device, Google Chrome may be your best bet, according to Apple.

To access iCloud Drive from a web browser, follow these steps:

1. **Open the browser and go to `www.icloud.com`.**
2. **Enter your Apple ID and click the arrow to the right.**
3. **Enter your Apple ID password and click the arrow to the right.**

   You're logged in to your iCloud account.
4. **Click the blue cloud icon (iCloud Drive) to access your stuff.**

Your iCloud Drive may look quite different from mine, which is shown in Figure 9-7. That's expected and okay. You will see folders, of course, but maybe not as many and not arranged in the same manner.

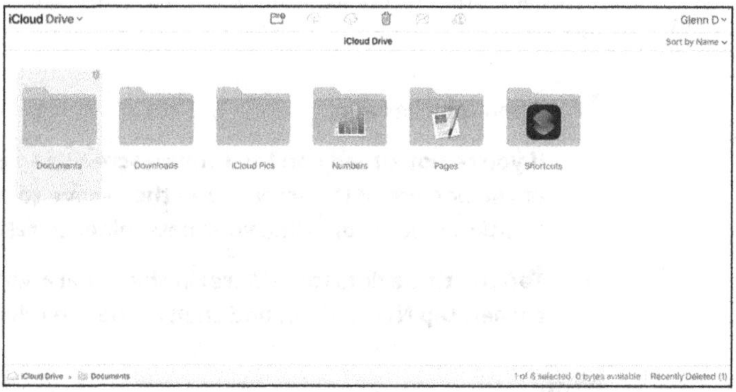
iCloud Drive
Glenn D
iCloud Drive
Sort by Name
Documents
Downloads
iCloud Pics
Numbers
Pages
Shortcuts

FIGURE 9-7: iCloud Drive as seen in iCloud.com.

Organizing Your Stuff

After you've enabled iCloud Drive access on your devices, you're ready to start storing things there. When it comes to storing files on a computer, smartphone, or tablet, you probably already know that folders are the key to good organization. The same is true for iCloud Drive, which utilizes folders as the primary way to keep things neat and tidy.

How you create folders and how you move things to and from iCloud Drive depend on how you're accessing it. Saving a file to iCloud Drive from an iPhone is a slightly different process than doing so from a Mac, for instance.

TIP

You may store any type of file you want in iCloud Drive, but regardless of file type, it must be 50GB or less.

Creating folders

Creating folders in iCloud Drive on your iPhone and iPad requires the use of the Files app. However, you create folders in iCloud Drive for Mac and Windows in the same way you do on your computer's hard drive.

iPhone and iPad

To create folders on an iPhone or iPad, use the Files app as follows:

1. **Open the Files app.**
2. **If you're not already on the Browse screen, tap Browse at the bottom of the screen, and then move to the location where you'd like your new folder to reside.**
3. **Tap the three dots icon (More) in the upper-right corner, tap New Folder, and then name the folder.**

Mac

To create a folder on a Mac, go to iCloud Drive in the left toolbar of the Finder window (as described earlier in this chapter). Then create a folder by using one of the following methods:

- Right-click or Control-click the area where you want to place the folder, select New Folder from the menu, and then name the folder.
- Move to the location where you want to create the new folder and press ⌘+Shift+N.
- In the Finder menu at the top of the screen, choose File ⇨ New Folder.

TIP

If you don't see the iCloud Drive option in the left toolbar of the Finder window, it may not be enabled in your Mac's Finder preferences. To enable iCloud Drive, make sure you're in Finder, click Finder next to the icon in the upper-left corner of your screen, and choose Preferences. Then click the Sidebar tab, and select the iCloud Drive option.

Windows

To create a folder in Windows, click iCloud Drive in the left toolbar of a File Explorer window (as described previously in this chapter). Then create a folder by using one of the following methods:

- Right-click the area where you want to place the folder and choose New ➪ Folder in the menu that appears, as shown in Figure 9-8. Then name the folder.
- Move to the location where you want to create the new folder and press Control+Shift+N.
- In the Home tab at the top of the File Explorer window, click the New Folder button.

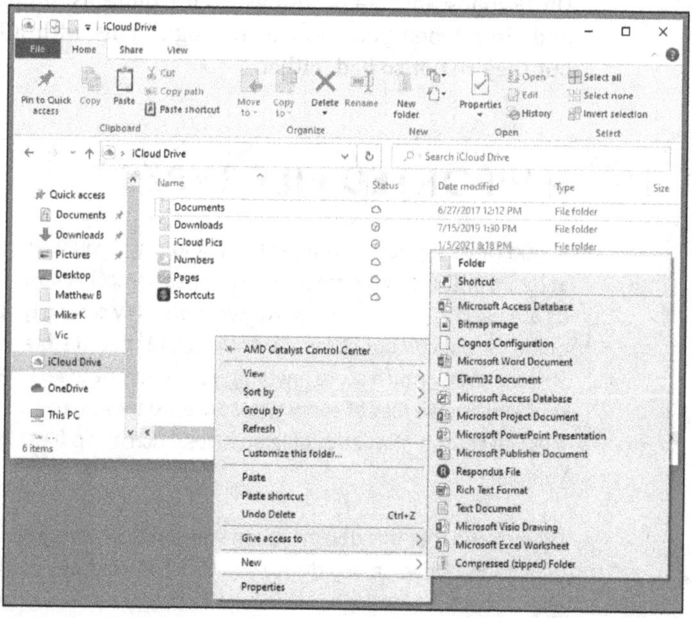

iCloud Drive
File
Home
Share
View
Pin to Quick access
Copy
Paste
Cut
Copy path
Paste shortcut
Clipboard
Move to
Copy to
Delete
Rename
Organize
New folder
New
Properties
Open
Edit
History
Select all
Select none
Invert selection
Select
iCloud Drive
Search iCloud Drive
Quick access
Documents
Downloads
Pictures
Desktop
Matthew B
Mike K
Vic
iCloud Drive
OneDrive
This PC
6 items
Name
Status
Date modified
Type
Size
Documents
Downloads
iCloud Pics
Numbers
Pages
Shortcuts
6/27/2017 12:12 PM
7/15/2019 1:30 PM
File folder
File folder
AMD Catalyst Control Center
View
Sort by
Group by
Refresh
Customize this folder...
Paste
Paste shortcut
Undo Delete
Ctrl+Z
Give access to
New
Properties
Folder
Shortcut
Microsoft Access Database
Bitmap image
Cognos Configuration
Microsoft Word Document
ETerm32 Document
Microsoft Access Database
Microsoft Project Document
Microsoft PowerPoint Presentation
Microsoft Publisher Document
Respondus File
Rich Text Format
Text Document
Microsoft Visio Drawing
Microsoft Excel Worksheet
Compressed (zipped) Folder

FIGURE 9-8: Creating a new folder using iCloud Drive for Windows.

iCloud.com

Finally, it's also wonderfully simple to create folders on iCloud.com:

1. **Sign in to iCloud.com.**
2. **Click the iCloud Drive button.**
3. **Move to the location where you want to create your new folder, if necessary.**
4. **Click the folder with a + icon (new folder), at the top of the window, and give your folder a good name.**

Managing folders and files

Folders are great, but only insofar as they actually store stuff, such as your files or other folders. As with creating folders, the steps necessary to work with files and folders in iCloud Drive differ depending on the device you're using.

iPhone and iPad

On iPhones and iPads, things aren't quite as simple as drag-and-drop when you want to manage items with iCloud Drive, but they're not so bad, either.

SUPPORTED FILE TYPES

iCloud Drive supports storage of any kind of file you want to throw at (or in) it. This may come as a surprise to some, because most of us are used to being told that we can store only certain types of files or file formats on our computers. With cloud-based storage, though, you can pretty much store anything your heart desires. PDFs? No problem. Image files of every type? Sure, go for it. Word and Excel files? Of course. How about file archives, such as zip files? Knock yourself out.

Understand that this doesn't mean you can open every file stored in your iCloud Drive on any device you use. For example, you won't be able to open a Mac Pages file using Word on your PC. But you will be able to store anything you please, as long as the file is 50GB or less.

TIP

You may be wondering how to save files from your apps into iCloud Drive. That's a good question, but the answer isn't simple because the steps can vary widely from app to app. In upcoming chapters, when you see how to use some apps such as Pages and Keynote, I discuss how to save files to iCloud Drive. That will at least give you a general idea of how to save files from apps to iCloud Drive.

To work with files and folders in the Files app, do the following:

1. **Open the Files app and navigate to the location of the file or folder you'd like to work with.**
2. **Tap-and-hold (long-press) the item.**

   The menu shown in Figure 9-9 appears.

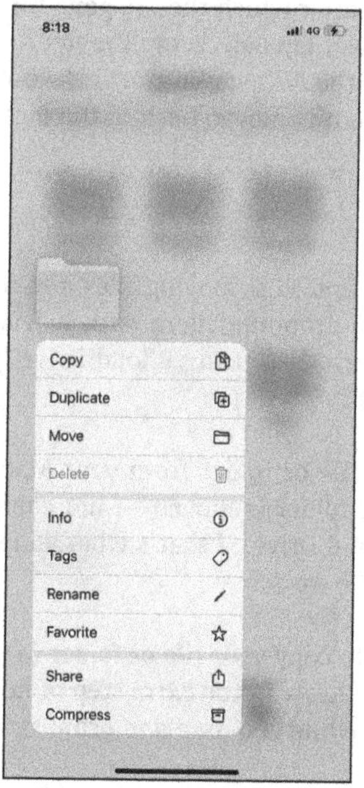
8:18
4G
Copy
Duplicate
Move
Delete
Info
Tags
Rename
Favorite
Share
Compress

FIGURE 9-9: A long-press reveals options you can take with an item.

3. **Tap an option to perform its corresponding action:**
   - *Copy:* Tap Copy to make an exact copy of the item in a different location. Then move to the location where you

want to copy the item, tap-and-hold the screen, and select Paste in the resulting menu.

- *Duplicate:* Tap Duplicate to make an exact copy of the item in the same location. The new item will appear with a 2 (or the next number if more than one duplicate is in the same location) after its name.
- *Move:* Tap Move to move the item to a different location. Then navigate to the new location and tap the Move button in the upper-right corner of the screen to complete the task.
- *Delete:* Tap Delete to toss the item in the trash.

TIP

Did you delete something by mistake? You can retrieve deleted items by tapping Browse at the bottom of the screen of the Files window, and then tapping the Recently Deleted button to see items you've deleted. (Items remain in the Recently Deleted folder for up to 30 days, after which they're gone for good.) Tap the three dots icon (More), tap Select, tap the item(s) you want to retrieve, and then tap the Recover button at the bottom of the screen. The recovered item is moved back to the location it was originally deleted from.

Mac and PC

When it comes to Macs and PCs, moving files and folders is as simple as dragging and dropping them with a few mouse or trackpad clicks. However, when using iCloud Drive, you should be a bit more intentional.

WARNING

If you drag and drop a file or folder from your Mac or PC into iCloud Drive, the file or folder is moved — not copied — from your computer into iCloud Drive. If that's what you want to do, great; all is right with the world.

However, if you meant to copy your file or folder (as opposed to moving it), you need to throw in the extra step of holding down a key on your keyboard while you drag and drop:

- For Mac, hold down the Option key while dragging and dropping the file or folder.
- For Windows, hold down the Ctrl key while dragging and dropping the file or folder.

VIEW YOUR MAC'S DESKTOP AND DOCUMENTS FILES ANYWHERE

iCloud Drive enables you to store files that reside on your Mac's desktop or Documents folder so you can share them with and access them from your other devices. For example, you could begin working on a file in your Mac's Documents folder, and then work on it later using your iPad. Go to the following page on Apple's Support website for more information on this great feature: `https://support.apple.com/en-us/HT206985`.

iCloud.com

iCloud Drive in iCloud.com is a tad more limited when it comes to working with files and folders, but it's still quite functional. For example, you can't move items to different locations, or even make copies of them. However, you can still upload and download files and folders, create new folders, and delete items.

Here are some tips for moving around and managing items (a few of which are shown in Figure 9-10) in iCloud Drive from iCloud.com:

- Double-click a folder to open it, or simply click its name (much like you'd click a link on a website).
- Upload files to a location by clicking the cloud with an upward-pointing arrow (at the top of the window), finding and selecting the file on your computer, and then clicking the Choose (Mac) or Open (Windows) button.
- Download a file from iCloud Drive to your computer by selecting it and then clicking the cloud with a downward-pointing arrow (at the top of the window).
- Delete a file or folder by selecting it and clicking the trash can icon (at the top of the window).

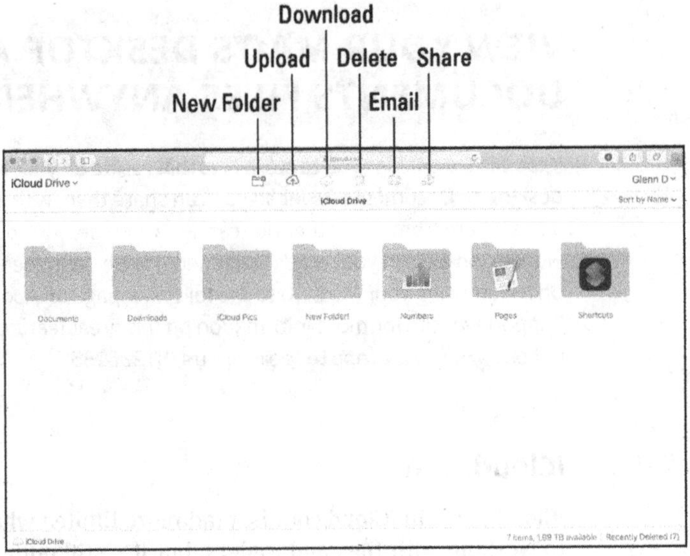
Download
Upload
Delete
Share
New Folder
Email
iCloud Drive
Glenn D
Sort by Name
Documents
Downloads
iCloud Pics
New Folder
Numbers
Pages
Shortcuts
Recently Deleted (7)

FIGURE 9-10: Note the icons at the top of the iCloud Drive window in iCloud.com.

TIP

Retrieve items you deleted by clicking Recently Deleted in the lower-right corner of the browser window. Select the item you want to retrieve, and then click Recover at the top of the window. The recovered item is moved back to the location it was originally deleted from. Items remain in the Recently Deleted folder for up to 30 days, after which they're permanently deleted.

your devices

» **Uploading, downloading, and sharing photos and videos**

Chapter 10
Picture This!

Photos and videos are ubiquitous these days. Everyone seems to have a smartphone and they use it to take photos and videos of everything from the most important life events to the silliest selfies they can conjure. (I'll be quite pleased when the dreaded "duck face" pose has ended its reign on social media.) The cameras on these things are amazing, allowing budding photogs to take pictures that would rival those taken with the very best photographic equipment from a decade or two ago.

However, the age-old problem of organization still exists. In the good ole days, photos were kept in albums or, worse, just tossed into boxes that were opened once in a blue moon. The digital age has ushered in another problem: The pictures you want are on a different device than the one you have handy. For goodness' sake, all we want is for our photos and videos to appear on every single device we own! Can anyone help us realize this goal?

"Why, yes," says Apple, "we can." iCloud Photos is just what the doctor ordered.

iCloud Photos stores your photos and videos in iCloud and enables you to sync them across your Apple devices and even Windows PCs.

Enable and Access iCloud Photos

In this section, you find out how to enable, access, and synchronize iCloud Photos on your devices. Something to remember: You'll need to be signed into your Apple ID on whatever devices you want to sync notes with: your iPhone, iPad, Mac, or Windows PC (using the iCloud for Windows app).

REMEMBER

Linux and Android users can access iCloud Photos only via a web browser through iCloud.com.

iCloud.com

All Apple One subscribers can access their photos and videos with the iCloud.com website's Photos app:

1. **Open a web browser and go to `www.icloud.com`.**
2. **Enter your Apple ID and password when prompted.**
3. **Click the Photos button to launch the web version of Photos.**

Apple devices

To sync photos and videos with your Apple devices, you must ensure that iCloud Photos is enabled on them. To enable syncing and to open the Photos app on your iPhone or iPad:

1. **Open the Settings app.**
2. **Tap your Apple ID at the top of the Settings list.**
3. **Tap iCloud and then tap Photos.**
4. **Tap the iCloud Photos switch to enable it (if it's not already enabled).**

5. **Leave the Settings app.**

   If your iPhone or iPad uses Face ID, swipe up to leave the app. If your iPhone or iPad has a Home button, press it to leave Settings.

6. **Tap to open the Photos app.**

To enable and access iCloud Photos on your Mac:

1. **Click in the top-left corner of your screen and select System Preferences.**
2. **Select Apple ID.**
3. **Select the box next to Photos to enable it, if it's not already selected.**
4. **Open your Applications folder, and double-click the Photos app icon to open it.**

Windows-based PC

You'll need the iCloud Drive app, which is available for Windows 10 by downloading it from the Microsoft Store. For more information, visit the "Download iCloud for Windows" article on Apple's Support site at `https://support.apple.com/en-us/HT204283`.

TIP

Be sure to set up your iCloud account on your Apple devices before you set it up on your PC.

After you've downloaded the iCloud for Windows app, do the following:

1. **Open the app.**
2. **Enter your Apple ID and password in the appropriate fields.**
3. **Click the Sign In button in the lower-right of the window.**
4. **Make sure the check box next to Photos is selected, and then click the Options button (shown in Figure 10-1).**
5. **Select iCloud Photos, click Done, and then click the Apply button in the lower right.**

iCloud
iCloud Drive
Photos
Options...
Mail, Contacts, Calendars, and Tasks
With Outlook
Bookmarks
Options...
iCloud
Dwight Spivey
a1fdummies@gmail.com
You have 5.00 GB of iCloud storage.
4.94 GB
Storage
Account details...
iCloud Help
Sign out
Apply
Close

FIGURE 10-1: Set up iCloud Photos using the iCloud for Windows app.

Working with iCloud Photos

Let's take a look at how to navigate the Photos app in its various forms. Photos in iCloud.com is simple but powerful. The Photos app for iOS behaves a bit differently than its cousins for macOS and iPadOS, so I've lumped the latter two together for our purposes in this part of the chapter.

REMEMBER

Edits you make in Photos for iOS, iPadOS, and macOS are reflected across all the devices you're signed into with your Apple ID.

iCloud.com

Photos for iCloud is easy to master but also offers some powerful features (for a web-based app) to help you do more than just dabble. Figure 10-2 shows you the Photos for iCloud interface.

Some options are self-explanatory, but others need a tad bit more info:

- **Sidebar:** Select an option to view your photos. You can view them all, by album, and by several other options, including Recently Deleted.
- **Share the selected file:** Click to share the file with others via a web link.

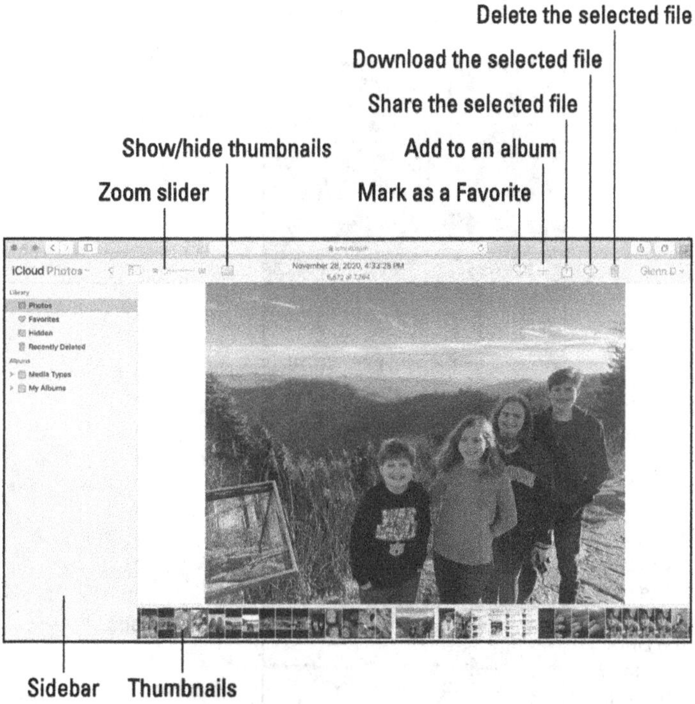

Delete the selected file
Download the selected file
Share the selected file
Show/hide thumbnails
Add to an album
Zoom slider
Mark as a Favorite
iCloud Photos
Sidebar
Thumbnails

FIGURE 10-2: Photos in iCloud.com is a great web-based app for photos and videos.

- **Download the selected file:** Click to save a full-resolution copy of the image to your computer.

TIP

Files in Recently Deleted are available for up to 30 days before being permanently vaporized.

The *iCloud User Guide* is chock-full of more information on the web version of Photos. Go to `https://support.apple.com/guide/icloud/welcome/icloud` and navigate to the Photos section to find out more than I can possibly cover in this chapter.

iOS

The Photos interface is necessarily different than other versions of the app due to the small-screen real estate on an iPhone. Some options and features are found in different locations than in other versions based on what you're viewing.

Figure 10-3 is the default view when you first open Photos for iOS.

Select files
More icon
7:35
Nov 25, 2020
Pigeon Forge
Select
Sort options
Years
Months
Days
All Photos
Tab bar

FIGURE 10-3: The main view from the Library tab in Photos for iOS.

Let's check out some of the options:

- **More icon:** The options available when you tap the More icon depend on the tab selected at the bottom of the screen and the sort option you've chosen.
- **Select:** Tap to put Photos into selection mode. Then tap photos or videos that you'd like to perform a simultaneous action on, such as selecting a set of photos to share with a friend or to delete in one fell swoop.
- **Tabs bar:** Tap an icon at the bottom of the screen to choose what you want to view in the Photos app. The Library icon shows all files you've stored on your device or in iCloud. The For You icon displays a tab with files curated based on things like location and people. Albums helps you organize photos and videos according to your liking. Search allows you to find files based on several criteria, such as name, people, places, and more.

Figure 10-4 gives you a different take: viewing a photo.

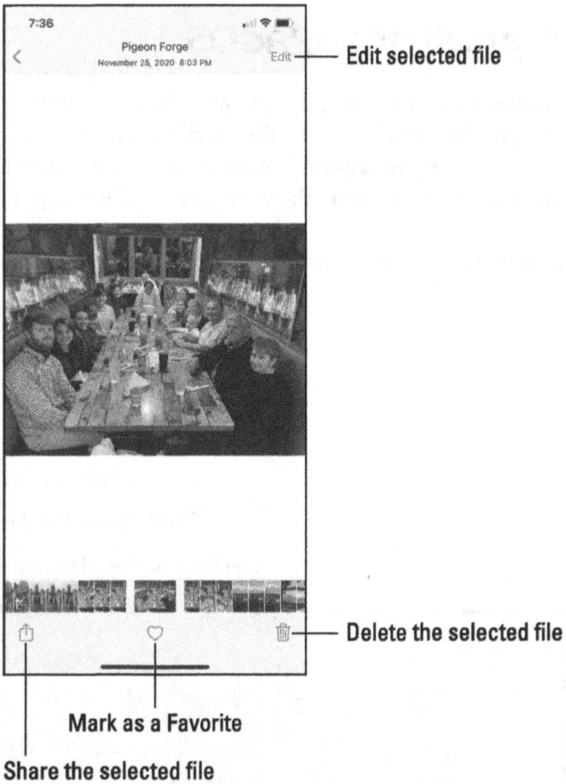
7:36
Pigeon Forge
November 25, 2020 8:03 PM
Edit
Edit selected file
Delete the selected file
Mark as a Favorite
Share the selected file

FIGURE 10-4: Viewing a picture in Photos for iOS.

Some of the options include the following:

- **Share the selected file:** Tap to share a copy of the photo or video with friends, family, enemies, or anyone else you'd like. You can share via apps such as Messages and Mail. This option also lets you create a slideshow, make duplicates, assign a photo to a contact, and much more.
- **Edit selected file:** Tap to open the edit window. From here you can make adjustments to color, contrast, and brightness. You can also rotate and crop photos.

The *iPhone User Guide* has much more information about using the options and features native to the Photos app for iOS. Check it out at `https://support.apple.com/guide/iphone/welcome/ios`.

macOS and iPadOS

Photos for macOS and iPadOS are similar enough that they can occupy the same space in this section. The iPad's larger screen allows the app to enjoy a feature layout similar to that of the Mac and (to a lesser extent) the web version of the app in iCloud.com.

Figure 10-5 is your Photos for macOS and iPadOS guide.

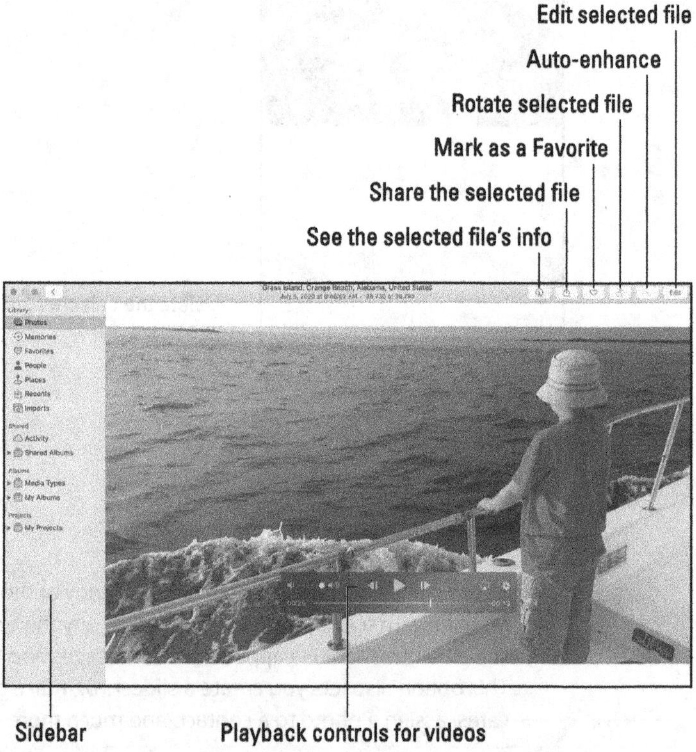

Edit selected file
Auto-enhance
Rotate selected file
Mark as a Favorite
Share the selected file
See the selected file's info
Sidebar
Playback controls for videos

FIGURE 10-5: Photos for macOS and iPadOS are similar in layout and options.

Some of these options deserve a bit of further attention:

- **See the selected file's info:** When you take a picture or video with your iPhone or iPad, much more information is stored than just the image itself. Some of that info includes the file type, the resolution the photo or video was shot with, the location it was captured, and much more that digital media nerds love to know about.

» **Auto-enhance:** Click or tap to allow Photos to make automatic adjustments to color, saturation, brightness, and more under-the-hood changes that enhance the look of your media files.

Check out the *macOS User Guide* at `https://support.apple.com/guide/mac-help/welcome/mac` to find out more about using Photos for macOS.

iPad afficionados will also want to inspect the *iPad Users Guide* at `https://support.apple.com/guide/ipad/welcome/ipados` to delve a bit deeper.

Windows-based PC

The iCloud for Windows app opens the door for your PC to sync photos and videos with iCloud and your Apple devices. There's much more I'd like you to know about iCloud Photos and Windows, and Apple has everything you need to know on their nifty Support site.

To learn more about how iCloud Photos works with Windows, including where files are saved, take a gander at this article on Apple's Support site called "Set up and use iCloud Photos on your Windows PC": `https://support.apple.com/en-us/HT205323`.

That wraps it up for this chapter. I hope you've learned a good deal about iCloud Photos, but it's a deep topic that bears further exploration if you're so inclined. Check out `https://support.apple.com/en-us/HT204570` to find answers to questions you may have and some you haven't thought of yet.

IN THIS CHAPTER

» Setting up an iCloud email account

» Sending, receiving, and replying to email

» Organizing your email

Chapter 11

You've Got (iCloud) Mail

I don't know about you, but I don't get much mail these days that isn't advertising. I won't lie . . . some days I wish good old-fashioned snail mail was still the main way to correspond. I kind of miss the anticipation (excitement, even?) of walking to the mailbox to retrieve the mail and not knowing what to expect. A letter from a friend? That thing-a-ma-bob I ordered weeks ago? The always-frightful unexpected bill? And after the mail was delivered, I didn't have to worry about anything new popping up until roughly 24 hours later, so I had time to enjoy (or perhaps recover from) what came today.

Those times are long gone, and it's probably for the best. Electron mail, a.k.a. email, has been all the rage for a while now, and it certainly has its advantages. The ability to instantly get in touch with someone is not a luxury I'm willing to part with, even for the halcyon days of snail mail.

If you have an Apple ID, you probably have an iCloud email account. If you don't, getting one is easy. In this chapter, you learn how to set up your iCloud email account on your devices, send and receive email, and organize your messages.

Setting Up iCloud Email

iCloud email is a free email service provided by Apple for anyone who has an Apple ID. Your iCloud email address can be the same as your Apple ID, but it doesn't have to be. For example, if you created your Apple ID using a Google email address (@gmail.com), you would have an iCloud email address with the @icloud.com suffix that looks like *your.name*@icloud.com.

REMEMBER

You're not limited to using only an iCloud email account if you have an Apple ID. The iCloud email account can be your default (main) email account or a secondary email account.

Creating an iCloud email address

You can create an iCloud email address when you create your Apple ID or later. (Because you've subscribed to Apple One, you already have an Apple ID.) If you didn't create an iCloud email address when you set up your Apple ID, just follow these steps, using your iPhone or iPad:

1. **Open the Settings app by tapping the gear icon.**
2. **At the top of the Settings list, tap your Apple ID.**
3. **Tap iCloud.**

   If the Mail switch is enabled (green), you already have an iCloud email account and should skip the remaining steps.
4. **If the Mail switch isn't enabled, tap it.**

   The Turn on Mail dialog appears, as shown in Figure 11-1.
5. **Tap Create.**
6. **Enter your preferred username in front of @icloud.com, and then tap Next in the upper-right corner to complete the process.**

To create an iCloud email address with your Mac, follow these steps:

1. **Click in the top-left corner of your screen and choose System Preferences.**

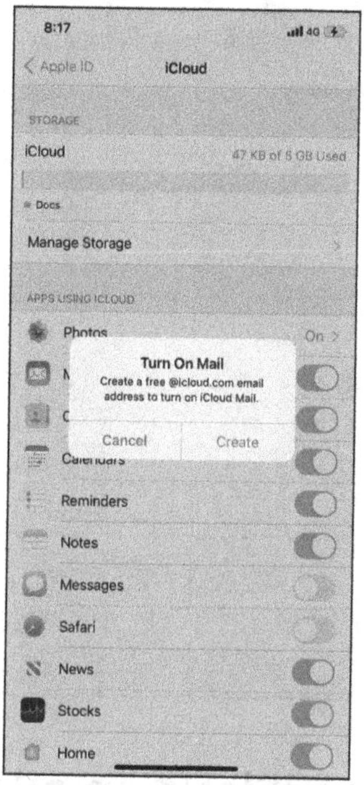
8:17
4G
Apple ID
iCloud
STORAGE
iCloud
47 KB of 5 GB Used
Docs
Manage Storage
APPS USING ICLOUD
Photos
On
Turn On Mail
Create a free @icloud.com email address to turn on iCloud Mail.
Cancel
Create
Reminders
Notes
Messages
Safari
News
Stocks
Home

FIGURE 11-1: Tap Create to create a new iCloud email address.

2. **Select Apple ID.**

   If the Mail option is selected, you have an iCloud email account and should skip the remaining steps.

3. **If the Mail check box is not selected, click it.**

   The Choose an iCloud Email Address dialog opens, as shown in Figure 11-2.

4. **Enter your preferred username in front of @icloud.com and then click the OK button to complete the process.**

TIP

If you're an Apple user from way back, you may already have an @me.com or @mac.com email address. If so, no worries: Apple has already created an equivalent @icloud.com address for you. For example, if your email address is *your.name*@mac.com, Apple's already created a *your.name*@icloud.com email address for you, whether you know it or not. You can continue to use your older addresses, too, without any problems.

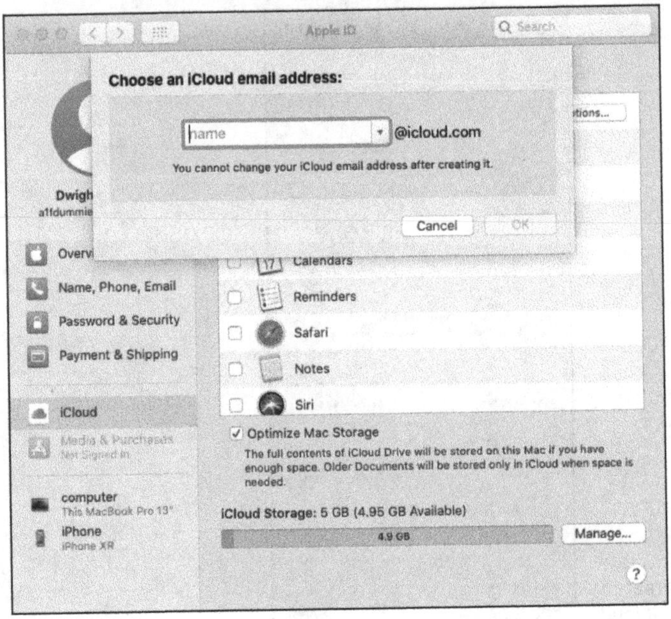
Choose an iCloud email address:
name
@icloud.com
You cannot change your iCloud email address after creating it.
Cancel
OK
Name, Phone, Email
Password & Security
Payment & Shipping
iCloud
computer
iPhone
iPhone XR
Calendars
Reminders
Safari
Notes
Siri
Optimize Mac Storage
The full contents of iCloud Drive will be stored on this Mac if you have enough space. Older Documents will be stored only in iCloud when space is needed.
iCloud Storage: 5 GB (4.95 GB Available)
4.9 GB
Manage...

FIGURE 11-2: Enter a username in front of @icloud.com.

Accessing your iCloud email

So, you have an iCloud email address. Now what? You need a way to see all those glorious communications.

Apple devices

It's super simple to access your iCloud email from your Apple devices, because Apple software and hardware work as seamlessly as possible.

To enable iCloud email and access it using your iPhone or iPad, do the following:

1. **Open the Settings app by tapping the gear icon.**
2. **At the top of the Settings list, tap your Apple ID.**
3. **Tap iCloud.**

4. **If the Mail switch is not green, tap it to enable it.**
5. **Exit the Settings app in one of the following ways:**
   - *If your iPhone or iPad uses Face ID,* swipe up on the screen. (If your device doesn't have a Home button, it uses Face ID.)
   - *If your iPhone or iPad has a Home button,* press it to exit Settings.
6. **Open the Mail app — your email will be ready and waiting.**

To enable iCloud email and access it using your Mac, follow these steps:

1. **Click in the top-left corner of the screen and select System Preferences.**
2. **Select Apple ID.**
3. **If the Mail option is not selected, click it to select it.**
4. **Go to Finder and press ⌘+Shift+A to open your Applications folder.**
5. **Double-click the Mail app icon to open Mail — you should see your iCloud email raring to go.**

Windows using Outlook

You can easily set up your iCloud email in Outlook on a Windows-based PC by using the iCloud for Windows app. If you have Windows 10, download and install the app from the Microsoft Store. If you have Windows 7 or 8, download the app from Apple's website by visiting `https://support.apple.com/en-us/HT204283`.

To set up iCloud email on Windows, do the following:

1. **Open the iCloud for Windows app.**
2. **Sign in using your Apple ID.**

3. **Select the Mail, Contacts, Calendars, and Tasks option, as shown in Figure 11-3, and then click Apply.**

   Your iCloud email settings are automatically applied to Outlook, and the Outlook app opens.

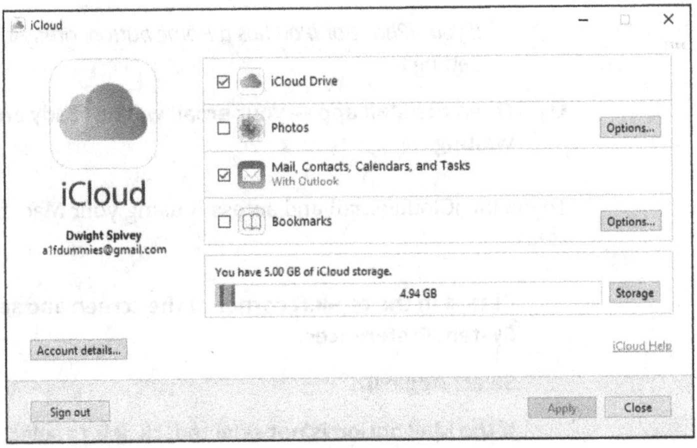

iCloud
iCloud Drive
Photos
Options...
Mail, Contacts, Calendars, and Tasks
With Outlook
Bookmarks
Options...
iCloud
Dwight Spivey
a1fdummies@gmail.com
You have 5.00 GB of iCloud storage.
4.94 GB
Storage
Account details...
iCloud Help
Sign out
Apply
Close

FIGURE 11-3: Setting up iCloud email for Outlook in Windows.

Third-party email apps

You can access your iCloud email on any of your devices also by using a third-party (or non-Apple) email app. However, you have to know which settings to use when adding your account to the device. Consult the instructions for the email app for details. Also visit Apple's Support site at `https://support.apple.com/en-us/HT202304` to get the necessary information for the incoming and outgoing mail servers.

iCloud.com

You can always access your iCloud email via the iCloud.com website's Mail app. Just follow these steps:

1. **Open a web browser and go to `www.icloud.com`.**
2. **Enter your Apple ID and password.**
3. **Click the Mail button to launch the web version of iCloud Mail, shown in Figure 11-4.**

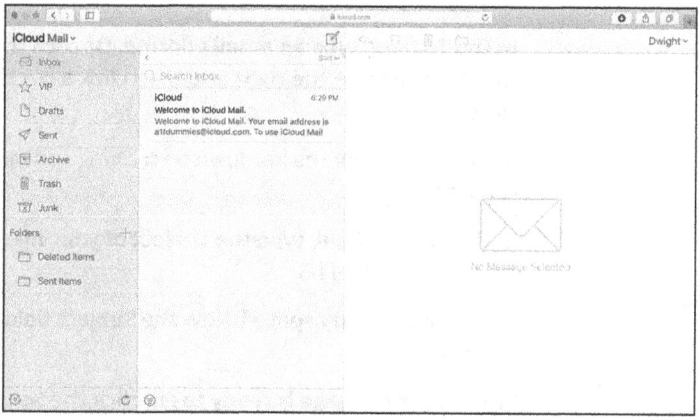
iCloud Mail
Inbox
VIP
Drafts
Sent
Archive
Trash
Junk
Folders
Deleted Items
Sent Items
Dwight
Search Inbox
iCloud
6:29 PM
Welcome to iCloud Mail.
Welcome to iCloud Mail. Your email address is
a11dummies@icloud.com. To use iCloud Mail
No Message Selected

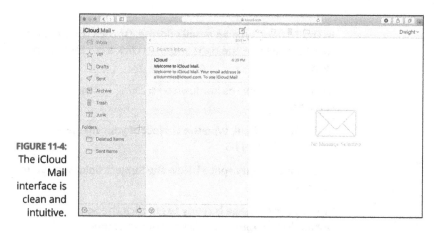

FIGURE 11-4: The iCloud Mail interface is clean and intuitive.

Sending and Receiving Email

From this point on in the chapter, I focus on using an iCloud email account with iCloud Mail in iCloud.com. Email apps such as Mail and Outlook, as well as third-party apps, have their own ways to go about the following tasks, and covering them is outside the scope of this book. Consult your email app's documentation for more information.

Mail in iCloud.com is a wonderfully simple app, and although it's not as powerful as most standalone email apps, it performs many functions quite well. The user-friendly and intuitive interface has generated very positive reviews.

TIP

Apple places some limitations ("safeguards," they call them) on iCloud Mail accounts, but these shouldn't hinder most users. For more information on these limitations, refer to the following article on Apple's Support site: `https://support.apple.com/en-us/HT202305`.

Creating and sending emails

To create and send an email with iCloud Mail, do the following:

1. **At the top of the Mail window, click the paper and pencil icon (compose) to open the Compose window.**

2. **In the To field, type an email address. Or click the circled + icon (contacts) to the right and then click a contact's name to select it.**

   See Chapter 13 for the lowdown on creating and managing contacts.

3. **In the Subject field, type the subject of your message, as shown in Figure 11-5.**
4. **In the large empty space below the Subject field, type your message.**
5. **When your message is ready to go, click the Send button in the upper-right corner of the Compose window.**

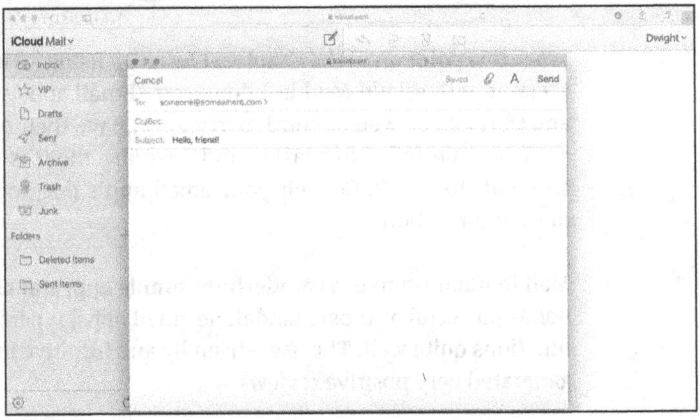
iCloud Mail
Dwight
Inbox
VIP
Drafts
Sent
Archive
Trash
Junk
Folders
Deleted Items
Sent Items
Cancel
Saved
Send
To: someone@somewhere.com
Cc/Bcc:
Subject: Hello, friend!

FIGURE 11-5: Enter email addresses and your subject in the appropriate fields.

Formatting emails

You can add attachments, such as pictures or other files, and you can also dress up your message by formatting the text.

To add an attachment, such as a picture or other file, do the following:

1. **If you're sending a picture, place your cursor where you want the picture to appear in the message.**
2. **Click the paperclip icon (attach a file) in the upper-right corner.**

3. **Browse your computer for the file you want to attach and then select it.**

   Pictures appear in-line with your message (at your cursor's location). Other types of files appear at the bottom of the message field. See Figure 11-6. You can click the Hide button in the lower right to hide the attachments; the button changes to More. Click the More button in the lower right to make the attachments visible again.

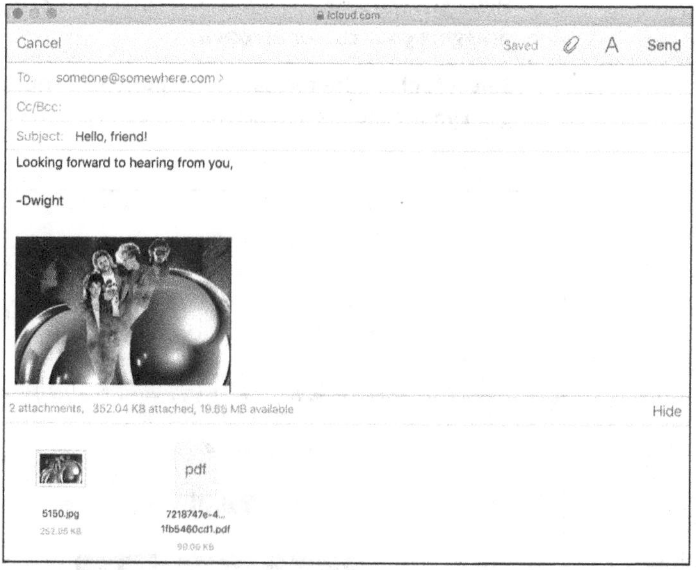
icloud.com
Cancel
Saved
A
Send
To: someone@somewhere.com >
Cc/Bcc:
Subject: Hello, friend!
Looking forward to hearing from you,
-Dwight
Hide
pdf
5150.jpg
7218747e-4...
1fb5460cd1.pdf

FIGURE 11-6: Attachments appear at the bottom of the Compose window.

Formatting the text of your message can jazz up whatever you need to say and make it more interesting to your reader. To manipulate your text, you use the format bar in the Compose window. The format bar offers several options:

- Select a different font, change the font's size, and adjust the font's color.
- Make the text bold, italic, or underlined.
- Align text to the left, center, or right.
- Add bullets or numbered lists.

» Toggle between indents or outdents for tabbing.
» Add hyperlinks for websites or email addresses.

To format the text of your message, do the following:

1. **In the upper-right corner of the Compose window, click the A icon (show format bar).**

   The format bar appears, as shown in Figure 11-7.

2. **Highlight the text you want to format by clicking and dragging your cursor across it.**

3. **Select tools in the format bar to punch up your text and grab your reader's attention.**

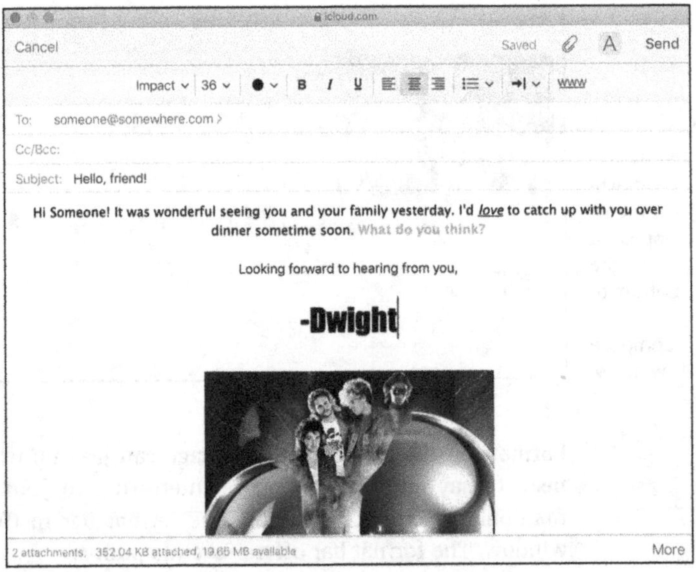
icloud.com
Cancel
Saved
A
Send
Impact
36
B
I
U
www
To: someone@somewhere.com
Cc/Bcc:
Subject: Hello, friend!
Hi Someone! It was wonderful seeing you and your family yesterday. I'd love to catch up with you over dinner sometime soon. What do you think?
Looking forward to hearing from you,
-Dwight
2 attachments, 352.04 KB attached, 19.65 MB available
More

FIGURE 11-7: The format bar allows you to gussy up your message text.

TIP

For more information on formatting text in your emails, visit `https://support.apple.com/guide/icloud/format-text-mm6b1a731d/icloud`.

Receiving and replying to email

Email that you receive is stored in Inbox, which is located in the Mail window. Back in the Stone Age, many office workers had an inbox and an outbox on their desks for work and correspondence they received or were sending, respectively, giving us the term *inbox* for the location of incoming emails.

To view and reply to emails you receive, follow these steps:

1. **In the left sidebar of the Mail window, select Inbox to see the list of emails it contains.**

   An unread email has a blue circle next to its subject.

2. **Click to select the email you want to view.**

   Its contents are displayed in the Message window on the right, as shown in Figure 11-8.

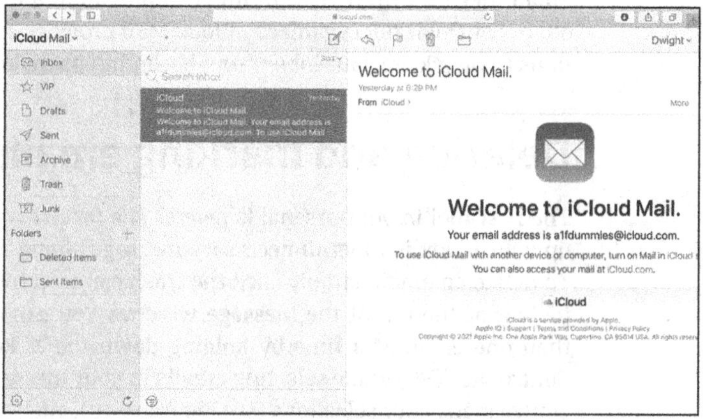
iCloud Mail
Inbox
VIP
Drafts
Sent
Archive
Trash
Junk
Folders
Deleted Items
Sent Items
iCloud
Dwight
Welcome to iCloud Mail.
From iCloud
More
Welcome to iCloud Mail.
Your email address is a1fdummies@icloud.com.
iCloud

FIGURE 11-8: The Message window displays your email.

3. **To reply to the email, click the left-pointing arrow icon (reply) in the menu bar at the top of the Message window and then select one of the following options (shown in Figure 11-9):**
   - *Reply:* Reply to the person who originally sent the email.
   - *Reply All:* Reply to everyone who received the email.
   - *Forward:* Send the email to someone who was not a recipient of the original email.

4. **Click Send in the upper-right corner of the Compose window.**

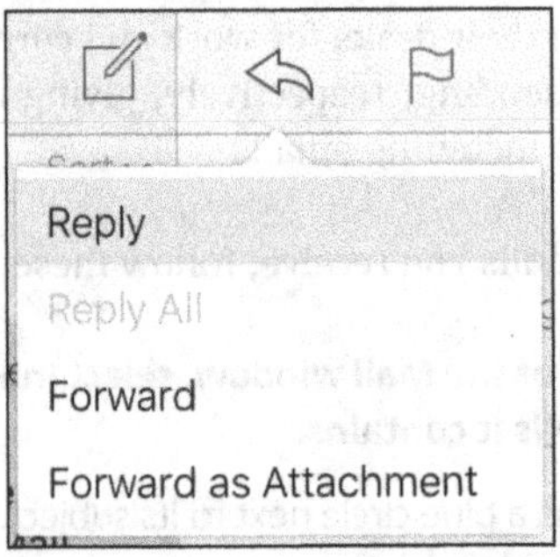
Reply
Reply All
Forward
Forward as Attachment

FIGURE 11-9: Click the reply icon to respond to or forward emails.

Organizing Email

Email, like everything else in life, can pile up in a hurry and get out of control if not organized. iCloud Mail provides several functions to help keep your inbox from becoming unwieldy.

Deleting and marking emails

The first tool in your arsenal is delete. The fastest way to clutter up your inbox is to let unnecessary messages hang around in it. To delete an email, simply click the trash can icon (delete) in the toolbar at the top of the Message window. You can delete more than one email at a time by holding down the ⌘ key (Mac) or Control key (PC) while selecting emails in your message list; once you've made your selections (see Figure 11-10), click the trash can icon to send them all packing.

TIP

You can retrieve emails you've deleted by selecting Trash in the left toolbar in the Mail window (refer to Figure 11-8). Locate and select the email you want to rescue from oblivion, click the folder icon (move to folder) in the toolbar at the top of the Message window, and then select a folder to move the email to (typically Inbox).

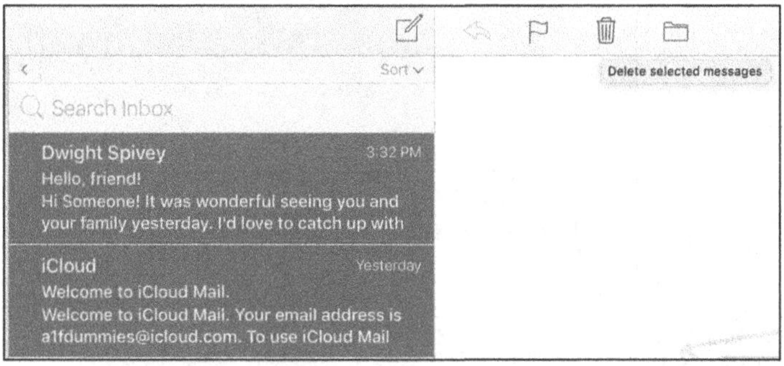
Sort
Delete selected messages
Search Inbox
Dwight Spivey
3:32 PM
Hello, friend!
Hi Someone! It was wonderful seeing you and your family yesterday. I'd love to catch up with
iCloud
Yesterday
Welcome to iCloud Mail.
Welcome to iCloud Mail. Your email address is a1fdummies@icloud.com. To use iCloud Mail

FIGURE 11-10: Delete emails individually or in batches.

You can also mark emails as read (or unread), flagged (or unflagged), or junk:

1. **Select one or more emails in your inbox.**

   To select multiple emails, hold down the ⌘ (Mac) or Control (PC) key while clicking.

2. **Click the flag icon in the toolbar at the top of the Message window and make your selection.**

   You can select Flag (or Unflag), Mark as Read (or Mark as Unread), or Junk, as shown in Figure 11-11.

REMEMBER

Junk emails are usually unsolicited advertisements. Marking an email as junk will cause future emails from the same sender to be automatically moved to the Junk folder.

Utilizing folders and rules

As with a good filing cabinet, you can use folders in Mail to organize messages by topics. Simply create a folder and place corresponding emails in it.

To create a folder, click the create a new mail folder icon (large +) next to Folders in the left toolbar of the Mail window and give it a name.

Place emails in a folder by clicking the move to folder icon (folder) in the toolbar at the top of the Message window and selecting the folder you want to move it to, as shown in Figure 11-12.

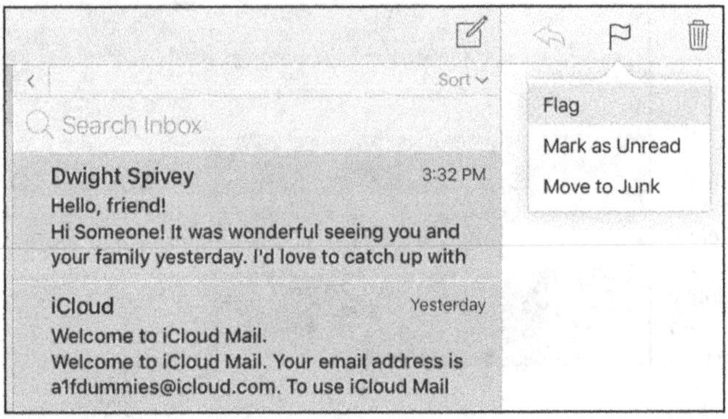
Sort
Search Inbox
Dwight Spivey
3:32 PM
Hello, friend!
Hi Someone! It was wonderful seeing you and your family yesterday. I'd love to catch up with
iCloud
Yesterday
Welcome to iCloud Mail.
Welcome to iCloud Mail. Your email address is a1fdummies@icloud.com. To use iCloud Mail
Flag
Mark as Unread
Move to Junk

FIGURE 11-11: Mark emails to help you keep track of them.

Hello, fri
9 minutes ago
From a1fdumm
Hi Someon
catch
Move to Folder
Inbox
Drafts
Sent
Archive
Trash
Junk
Deleted Items
Sent Items
Work

FIGURE 11-12: Move emails to folders to organize them.

If moving emails one a time is too tedious, or you'd like to automate the process, Mail enables you to create rules for your incoming email messages. Follow these steps to create a rule:

1. **Click the gear icon (Actions menu) in the lower-left corner of the Mail window and then select Rules.**
2. **Click Add a Rule in the upper-right corner of the Rules window.**

3. **In the If a Message section, select an action in the drop-down menu.**
4. **In the Then section, select a consequence on the first and second drop-down menus (see Figure 11-13).**
5. **To add the new rule to the Rules list, click Done.**

ion
Rules
If a message
is from
Dwight
Then
Move to Folder
Work
Cancel
Done
Add a Rule...
anize your mail with Rules.
Done

FIGURE 11-13: Actions have consequences!

To modify or delete a rule, click the circled *i* icon (info) to the right of the rule, as shown in Figure 11-14.

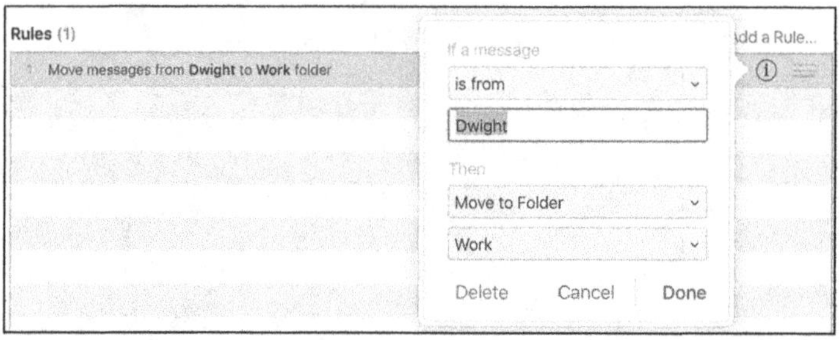
Rules (1)
1 Move messages from Dwight to Work folder
If a message
is from
Dwight
Then
Move to Folder
Work
Delete
Cancel
Done
dd a Rule...

FIGURE 11-14: Rules are easy to modify or delete.

iCloud Mail is a good web-based email app, and now you have the know-how to use it to work with your email from any Internet-connected computer. Although iCloud Mail can't jump through as many hoops as a dedicated email app (such as Mail or Outlook), it's more than capable of handling most of your needs. There's plenty more to learn about iCloud Mail, so don't be shy about visiting the *iCloud User Guide* for more information at `https://support.apple.com/guide/icloud/welcome/icloud`.

IN THIS CHAPTER

» Accessing the Calendar and Reminders apps

» Add and delete calendar events

» Make, edit, and delete reminders and lists

Chapter 12

Tying a Digital String on Your Finger

I'm not the most organized of individuals, and I used to rely on a Day-Timer to keep track of my days, which start early and end late. If I didn't have a way to keep track of my comings and goings, I'd be a very unpopular fellow. Between school schedules, sports schedules, work schedules, doctors' appointments, and everything else going on, I need help keeping it all straight — otherwise, it spins out of control.

But now, instead of a Day-Timer, I use the Calendar and Reminders apps to keep everything in one place: iCloud.

Calendar is exactly what you think it is — an online version of the monthly calendar we've all hung on our office or kitchen walls at one time or another. The only feature of a paper calendar that you might miss are the nice pictures; you'll need to look elsewhere for those if you're using Calendar on your iPhone or Mac.

Reminders is the to-do list we all wish we had 20 years ago. One that can be found in one place (or in all places, depending on how you look at it) and that doesn't get ruined if you accidentally leave it in your pants pocket while washing your clothes.

In this chapter, you find out how to access and use both Calendar and Reminders on your devices. And yes, those devices include both Apple and non-Apple contraptions.

The Dating Game: Getting to Know Calendar

Calendar is a free calendar service provided by Apple for anyone who has an Apple ID. Your Apple ID is what keeps everything tied together, so that events are synced with little fuss or muss. You sign in with your Apple ID on every device you want to use with Calendar, and whatever changes you make on one will be reflected on all the rest. So, if you add an event in Calendar using iCloud.com, the event will immediately appear in Calendar on your iPad, as long as both devices are signed into the same Apple ID.

REMEMBER

You're not limited to using only an Apple ID with Calendar. You can use other calendar services, such as Google or Outlook, with the Calendar app on your Apple devices, which I discuss later in this chapter. However, you will see only your iCloud calendars in iCloud.com.

Accessing Calendar

I'm about to show you how to enable and access Apple Calendar on your devices. One thing to remember: You need to be signed into your Apple ID on your iPhone, iPad, Mac, or into the iCloud for Windows app. If you need a refresher, please head back to Chapter 8.

Apple devices

The first step in using Calendar is to make sure syncing it is enabled on your Apple devices, which makes your calendars accessible in the Calendar app and in other third-party calendar apps.

To enable Calendar syncing using your iPhone or iPad:

1. **Open the Settings app.**
2. **Tap your Apple ID at the top of the Settings list.**
3. **Tap iCloud.**
4. **If the Calendars switch isn't enabled, tap it to enable it.**
5. **If your iPhone or iPad uses Face ID, swipe up on the screen to leave the Settings app.**

   If your iPhone or iPad has a Home button, press it to leave Settings.
6. **Tap to open your Calendar app.**

   Your calendars and events are displayed.

To enable Calendar syncing on your Mac:

1. **Click in the top-left corner of your screen and select System Preferences.**
2. **Select Apple ID or choose Internet Accounts ⇨ iCloud.**
3. **Select the box next to Calendars to enable it, if it's not already selected.**
4. **Open your Applications folder.**
5. **Double-click the Calendar app icon to open it.**

Windows using Outlook

Outlook is a great app that includes a calendar function that will work with Apple Calendar. If you're using Windows 10, download and install the iCloud for Windows app from the Microsoft Store. If you have Windows 7 or 8, download the app from Apple's website by visiting `https://support.apple.com/en-us/HT204283`.

To set up Apple Calendar on Windows:

1. **Open the iCloud for Windows app and sign in with your Apple ID.**

2. **Select the Mail, Contacts, Calendars, and Tasks box, and then click Apply.**

   Your Calendar settings automatically sync with Outlook and the Outlook app opens.

Third-party calendar apps

You can use third-party (non-Apple) calendar apps on your devices to access your Apple Calendar calendars, but how you go about doing so is strictly up to the app. Check the instructions provided by the app developer to learn how to set this up. Some popular apps that come to mind are Google Calendar, Fantastical, Woven, and the aforementioned Outlook (see the preceding section).

iCloud.com

As always, you can access your Apple Calendar calendars with the iCloud.com website's Calendar app:

1. **Open a web browser and go to `www.icloud.com`.**
2. **Enter your Apple ID and password when prompted.**
3. **Click the Calendar button to launch the web version of Calendar.**

Working with Calendar in iCloud.com

Calendar apps, including Apple Calendar and those from other parties, have their various ways of working with events. I advise checking the documentation of your preferred app for more information. From here, I concentrate on using Calendar in iCloud.com.

Getting around in Calendar

You need to know the lay of the land to get the most out of Calendar. Luckily, it's a simple interface that makes it super-easy to get around.

When you open Calendar, your window will look similar to mine, which is shown in Figure 12-1.

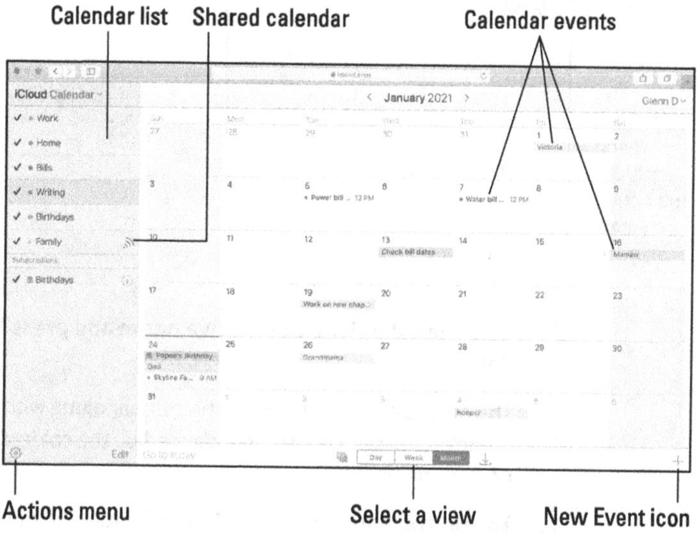
Calendar list
Shared calendar
Calendar events
Actions menu
Select a view
New Event icon

FIGURE 12-1: Get to know Calendar's layout.

Things to note:

- **Each calendar is assigned a unique color.** Events created for a calendar use the same color to help you stay organized.
- **Click the Day, Week, or Month button to change your Calendar view.**
- **Click the area to the left of a calendar to display or hide it and its events.** A check mark indicates that the calendar's events are displayed.

TIP

You can rearrange calendars in the left sidebar of the window by dragging them up or down the list and then dropping them where you want them to go.

Creating and editing calendars

To create and edit a calendar in iCloud.com's Calendar app:

1. **Click the gear icon (Actions) in the lower-left of the sidebar and choose New Calendar, as shown in Figure 12-2.**

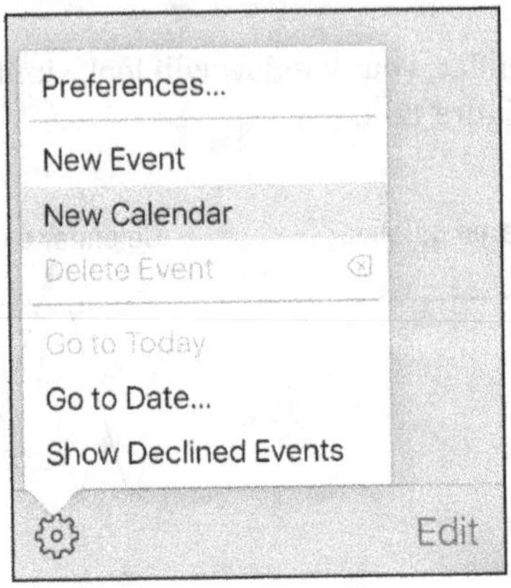
Preferences...
New Event
New Calendar
Delete Event
Go to Today
Go to Date...
Show Declined Events
Edit

FIGURE 12-2: The Actions menu includes the option to create a calendar.

2. **Give the calendar a descriptive name and press Enter or Return.**

   The new calendar appears in the sidebar along with the others. It's assigned a color, indicated by the colored dot next to the name.

3. **To edit the name or color of the calendar, click the Edit button at the bottom of the sidebar, and then do one or both of the following:**

   - *To change the name, click it and type a new one. Press Enter or Return to apply the change.*
   - *To edit the calendar's color, click the colored dot next to the name and click a new color to select it (see Figure 12-3).*

4. **To complete your changes, click Done at the bottom of the sidebar.**

Share your calendars

Sharing calendars allows others to see your schedule and also helps coordinate activities with groups. To share a calendar:

1. **Click the share icon to the right of a calendar in the sidebar.**

   The Share icon is labeled in Figure 12-1.

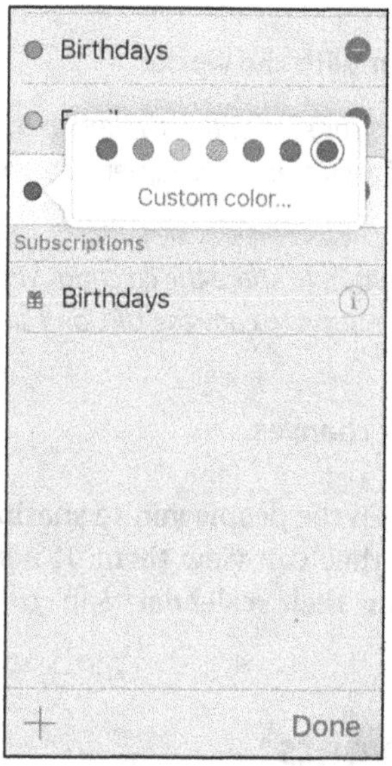
Birthdays
Custom color...
Subscriptions
Birthdays
Done

FIGURE 12-3: Select a color for your new calendar.

2. **To share your calendar with specific iCloud users:**

   a. Select Private.

   b. Enter the name, email address, or phone number of the person you want to add in the Add Person field. Continue to add as many people as necessary.

   c. Change a user's privileges by clicking the tiny arrow next to the person's name and selecting View & Edit or View Only, as shown in Figure 12-4.

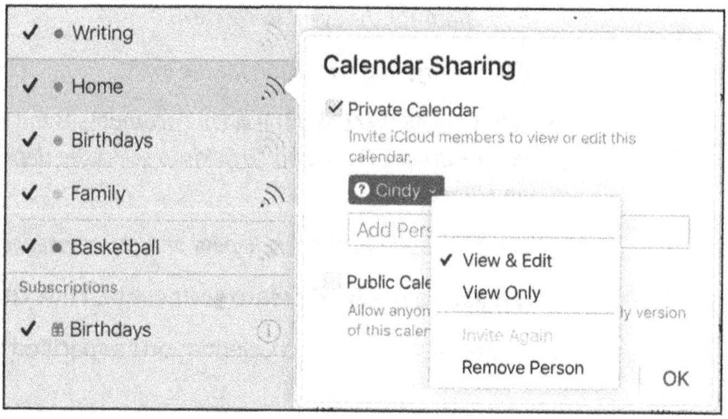
Writing
Home
Birthdays
Family
Basketball
Subscriptions
Birthdays
Calendar Sharing
Private Calendar
Invite iCloud members to view or edit this calendar.
Cindy
View & Edit
View Only
Invite Again
Remove Person
OK

FIGURE 12-4: Assigning privileges to a user in a privately shared calendar.

3. **To share your calendar with the world:**

   a. *Select Public Calendar from the options.* A link to a read-only version of the calendar is generated and displayed.

   b. *Click the Email Link button to share the calendar via email or click the Copy Link button to copy the URL and share it in some other fashion.*

4. **Click OK to apply your changes.**

TIP

It's a good idea to check with the people you're sharing your calendars with to make sure they can view them. If not, they may need to do something in their calendar app to view your calendars.

Create calendar events

Having an empty calendar does no one any good, so what you need to do next is add some events. To create new calendar events:

1. **Click the + icon (new event) in the lower-right of the Calendar window.**

   The + icon is labeled in Figure 12-1.

2. **In the New Event window (shown in Figure 12-5), do the following:**

   a. *In the New Event field at the top, add a name for your event.*

   b. *Click the colored dot to the right of the event name to select a calendar for the event to reside in.*

   c. *If necessary, add a location for the event.*

   d. *Select the All Day box if the event encompasses the entire day, or use the From and To fields to select the desired dates and times.*

   e. *Set other options, such as Repeat or Alert, as needed.*

3. **When you're ready to create your event, click OK.**

   The new event appears in Calendar on its specified date.

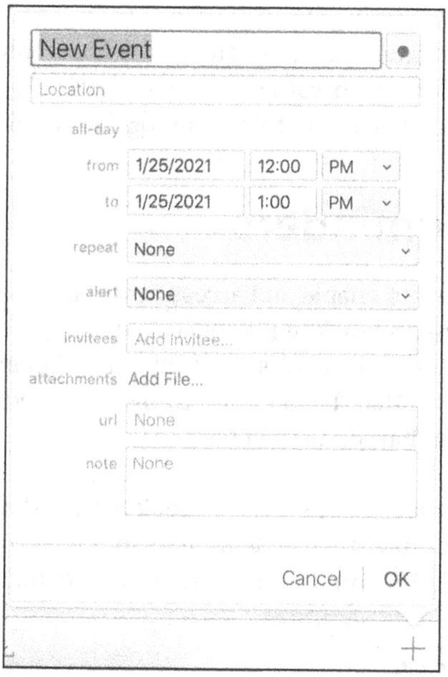
New Event
Location
all-day
from 1/25/2021 12:00 PM
to 1/25/2021 1:00 PM
repeat None
alert None
invitees Add invitee...
attachments Add File...
url None
note None
Cancel
OK

FIGURE 12-5: A new event window is where the magic happens.

To delete an event, simply double-click it and click the red Delete button in the lower-left corner of the event's options window.

TIP

You can make adjustments to some Calendar features by changing the app's Preferences to your liking. To check out the available options, click the gear icon (Actions menu) in the lower-left corner of the sidebar and select Preferences. Click Save to apply any changes you make.

Remind Me, Again, Please!

Let's face it, we all need help remembering things from time to time. And if your household holds more than just you (I have six people in my house), there's a lot more to remember. Apparently, some good folks at Apple have similar needs and created a nifty software tool called Reminders.

Reminders is yet another Apple creation whose name tells you exactly what it lives and breathes for (metaphorically speaking, of course): to remind you of anything you need reminding of.

Access Reminders

Let's find out how to enable and access Apple Reminders on your devices. And here's a quick reminder (yes, indeed, the pun is very much intended): You must be signed into your Apple ID on your iPhone, iPad, and Mac. If you need to be reminded (there I go again) how to do that, go to Chapter 8.

REMEMBER

Reminders no longer works with Outlook for Windows as of iOS 13. However, you may still use Reminders in iCloud.com from any Internet-connected computer, so Windows users take heart.

Apple devices

You'll want to make sure that Reminders syncing is enabled on all your Apple devices, so you can see and sync your reminders easily no matter which device you're currently using.

To enable syncing for Reminders on your iPhone or iPad:

1. **Open the Settings app.**
2. **Tap your Apple ID at the top of the Settings list.**
3. **Tap iCloud.**
4. **Tap the Reminders switch to enable it, if necessary, as shown in Figure 12-6.**

   When enabled, the switch appears green.
5. **Exit the Settings app.**

   If your iPhone or iPad uses Face ID, swipe up on the screen to leave the Settings app. If your iPhone or iPad has a Home button, press it to exit Settings.
6. **Open your Reminders app to see your upcoming tasks.**

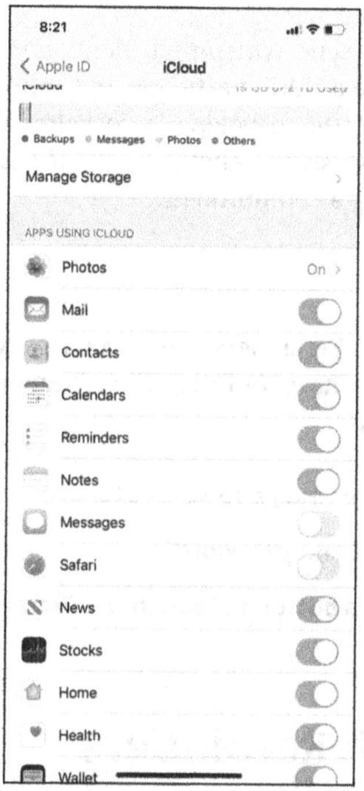
8:21
Apple ID
iCloud
Backups
Messages
Photos
Others
Manage Storage
APPS USING ICLOUD
Photos
On
Mail
Contacts
Calendars
Reminders
Notes
Messages
Safari
News
Stocks
Home
Health
Wallet

FIGURE 12-6: Toggle the Reminders switch to enable it on your iPhone or iPad.

To enable syncing for Reminders on your Mac:

1. **Click in the top-left corner of your screen and select System Preferences.**
2. **Select Apple ID or choose Internet Accounts ⇨ iCloud.**
3. **Select the box next to Reminders to enable it, if necessary.**
4. **Open your Applications folder.**
5. **Double-click the Reminders app icon to open it.**

Third-party task and to-do apps

You can use third-party (non-Apple) task (or to-do) apps on your devices, but how you use them and set up your accounts in them is different from app to app. Some popular task apps are GoodTask, Google Tasks, Things, and MinimaList.

TIP

Some third-party apps sync with Apple Reminders and some don't. If you want to use a third-party app and continue to sync with Reminders, check the developer's website or do some research on your favorite search engine to see if that feature is supported before making a commitment.

iCloud.com

iCloud.com also houses a Reminders app so you can stay on point with tasks anywhere you have an Internet connection. To access Reminders on iCloud.com:

1. **Open a web browser and go to `www.icloud.com`.**
2. **Enter your Apple ID and password.**
3. **Click the Reminders button to launch the Reminders web app.**

Working with Reminders

Regardless of which device or platform you use to access the Reminders app, it works almost the same. You can perform the same functions in almost the same manner on an iPhone, an iPad, or a Mac.

However, Reminders in iCloud.com is so super-simple it's surprising. No kidding, you can perform only a handful of tasks in the web app, and those are as basic as basic can get:

» **View lists and reminders.** It doesn't get more basic than that.

» **Create a new (barebones) reminder.** By *barebones*, I mean that you can't flag the reminder, assign a priority to it, or add a due date for it. You can only name it and add some notes.

» **Edit the title of a reminder and its notes.**

» **Mark a reminder as complete or incomplete.**

» **Edit the name and appearance of a list.**

» **Show or hide completed reminders.**

Creating and editing lists

Lists are to the Reminders app what folders are to filing cabinets. Create lists for various areas or interests of your life, and then add reminders to those lists to keep things organized. For example, you might have a list for work and another for home.

TIP

The default list is shockingly (he said sarcastically) named Reminders. It's basically a catch-all for reminders for which you haven't or don't want to create a list.

To create and edit a new list in the Reminders app for iOS and iPadOS:

1. **Tap Add List in the lower-right corner of the My Lists screen (the main screen in the Reminders app) to open the Name & Appearance screen.**

   Tap Lists in the upper-left corner if you're not on the My Lists screen when you open Reminders.

2. **Give the list a descriptive name.**
3. **Select a color and icon for the list by tapping the available options, as shown in Figure 12-7, and then tap Done.**
4. **If you want to change the name or appearance of the list:**

   a. *Tap the list to select it in the My Lists screen.*

   b. *Tap the three blue dots icon (More) in the upper-right corner, and then tap Name & Appearance in the menu that appears.*

   c. *Tap Done.*

To create and edit a new list in the Reminders app for macOS:

1. **To create a list, select Add List in the lower-left corner of the My Lists sidebar.**
2. **Give the list a descriptive name.**
3. **If you want to change the icon representing the list, click the list's icon in the sidebar and make your changes, as shown in Figure 12-8.**

   You can also rename the list at this time.

4. **Select OK when you're done.**

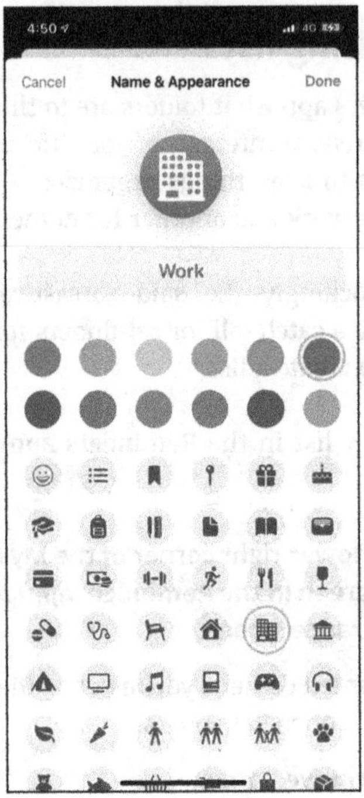
4:50
Cancel
Name & Appearance
Done
Work

FIGURE 12-7: Customizing a list's name and appearance in iOS.

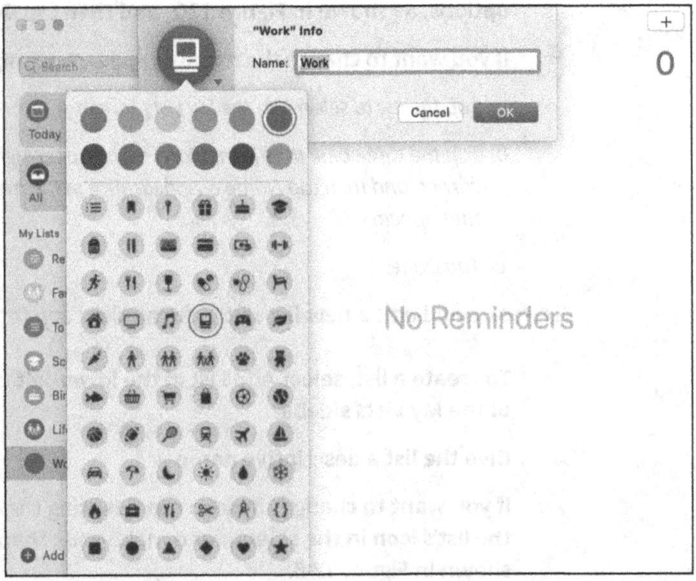
"Work" Info
Name:
Work
Cancel
OK
Today
All
My Lists
No Reminders
0
Add

FIGURE 12-8: Editing a list's name and icon in macOS.

REMEMBER

You can't create new lists in iCloud.com.

Creating and editing reminders

Reminders are simply items or actions you'd like help remembering to complete. To create and edit reminders for iOS and iPadOS:

1. **Tap New Reminder in the lower-left corner of the screen.**
2. **Enter a descriptive title for the reminder and add some notes if you'd like in the appropriately named Title and Notes fields.**
3. **Tap Details and then toggle the appropriate switches to green to add any of the following to your reminder:**
   - *Date:* Select a date from the calendar.
   - *Time:* Enter a time (and don't forget to set AM or PM!).
   - *Location:* The reminder notification opens when you arrive at a specific location, as shown in Figure 12-9.
   - *When Messaging:* The reminder notification opens when you're involved in a conversation with someone in the Messages app.
   - *Flag:* Flags help an especially important reminder stand out from the rest.
   - *Priority:* This option helps you know how urgent the reminder is.
   - *Image:* Add an image for your task.
   - *URL:* Add a link to a website related to the task.
4. **Tap New Reminder in the upper left.**
5. **Tap Lists and tap the list in which you want the reminder to reside.**
6. **When you're finished, tap Add in the upper right of the New Reminder window.**

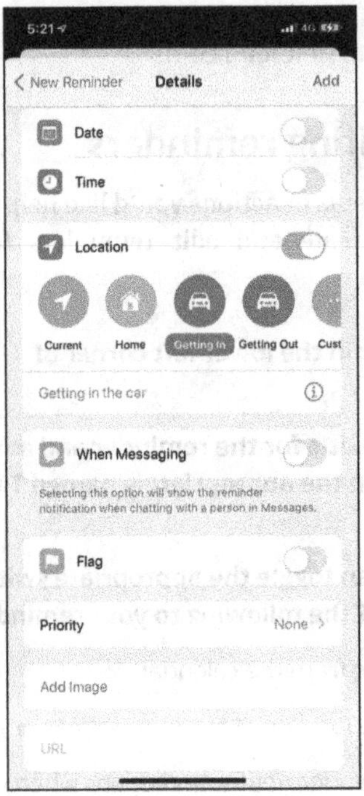
5:21
New Reminder
Details
Add
Date
Time
Location
Current
Home
Getting In
Getting Out
Cust
Getting in the car
When Messaging
Selecting this option will show the reminder notification when chatting with a person in Messages.
Flag
Priority
None
Add Image
URL

FIGURE 12-9: Add details to your reminder for scheduling and organizing.

To create and edit reminders for macOS:

1. **Select a list for the reminder from the My Lists sidebar.**
2. **Select the large + in the upper-right corner of the selected lists window.**
3. **Give the list a descriptive name and enter any notes you deem necessary.**
4. **Select the Information button to the right of the new reminder if you'd like to add any of the following to it:**
   - *Flag* (in the upper-right corner)
   - *Remind Me on a Day:* See Figure 12-10.
   - *Remind Me at a Time*
   - *Remind Me at a Location:* The reminder notification opens when you arrive at a specific location.
   - *Remind Me when Messaging a Person:* The reminder notification opens when you're involved in a conversation with someone in the Messages app.

- *Repeat:* Choose an interval if needed.
- *Priority*
- *URL:* Add a link to a website related to the task.
- *Image:* Add an image for your task.

5. **Click anywhere outside the details window to finish.**

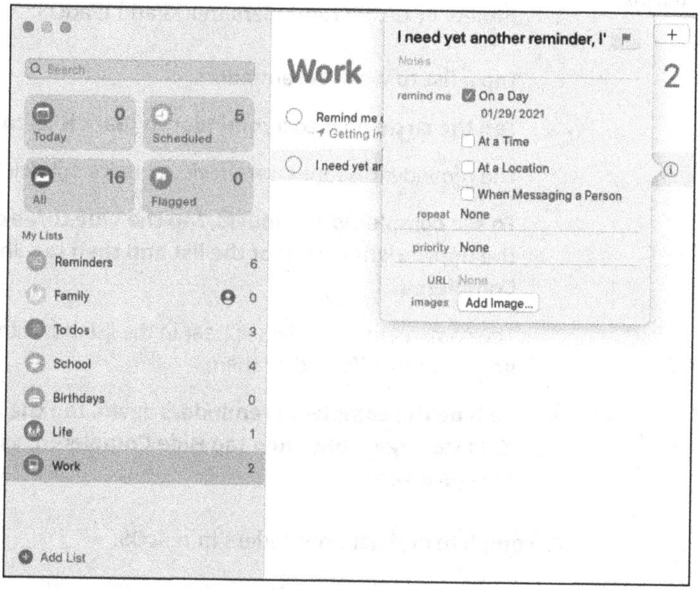
Today
0
Scheduled
5
All
16
Flagged
0
My Lists
Reminders
6
Family
0
To dos
3
School
4
Birthdays
0
Life
1
Work
2
Add List
Work
2
Remind me
Getting in
I need yet ar
I need yet another reminder, I'
Notes
remind me
On a Day
01/29/ 2021
At a Time
At a Location
When Messaging a Person
repeat
None
priority
None
URL
None
images
Add Image...

FIGURE 12-10: Adding details in Reminders for macOS.

To create and edit reminders in iCloud.com:

1. **In the left sidebar, select a list where you want to keep the reminder.**
2. **Click the New Reminder button at the bottom of the window.**
3. **Give the reminder a descriptive name, add some notes if you need to, and then click anywhere on the screen.**

REMEMBER

While you can view reminder details you created in Reminders for iOS, iPadOS, or macOS in iCloud.com, you can't add or edit reminder details in iCloud.com.

Complete or delete reminders

Marking a reminder as complete removes it from view in your list (although you can view completed reminders if need be). Deleting a reminder gets rid of it for good.

WARNING

You cannot retrieve a deleted reminder. When I say they're gone for good, I mean they're gone for good.

To complete or delete reminders in iOS and iPadOS:

1. **Tap a list to view its reminders.**
2. **Tap the circle next to a reminder to mark it as completed.**

   The reminder disappears from view, but it's not deleted.
3. **To see completed reminders, tap the blue three dots icon in the upper-right corner of the list and then tap Show Completed.**

   The completed reminders appear in the list, but with a light gray color to differentiate them.
4. **To hide the completed reminders again, tap the three dots icon again and then tap Hide Completed, as shown in Figure 12-11.**

To complete or delete reminders in macOS:

1. **In the My Lists sidebar, select a list to see its reminders.**
2. **Select the circle next to a reminder to mark it complete.**

   The reminder disappears, but it's not deleted.
3. **To see completed reminders, scroll to the top of the list until you see the number of reminders that have been completed, and then select Show (to the right).**

   The completed reminders appear in the list, but with a light gray color to differentiate them.
4. **To hide the completed reminders again, scroll to the top of the list until you see the number of reminders that have been completed, and then select Hide (to the right), as shown in Figure 12-12.**

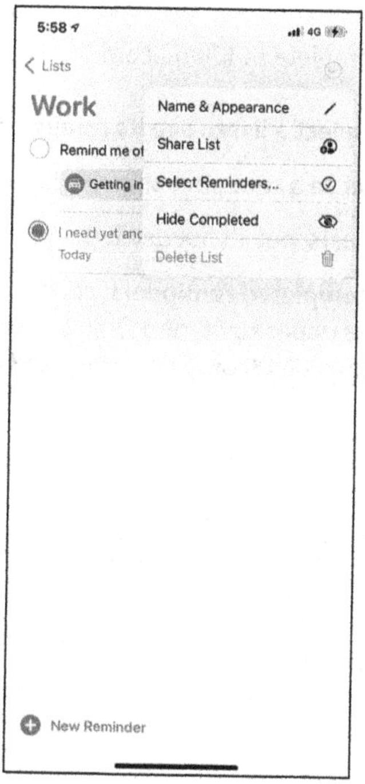
5:58
4G
Lists
Work
Name & Appearance
Share List
Select Reminders...
Hide Completed
Delete List
Remind me of
Getting in
I need yet anc
Today
New Reminder

FIGURE 12-11: Hiding completed reminders in iOS.

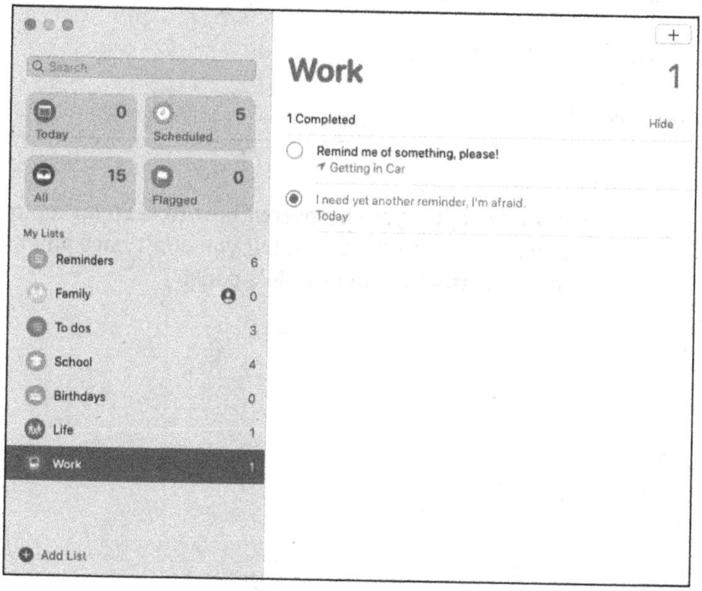
Search
Today
0
Scheduled
5
All
15
Flagged
0
My Lists
Reminders
6
Family
0
To dos
3
School
4
Birthdays
0
Life
1
Work
1
Add List
+
Work
1
1 Completed
Hide
Remind me of something, please!
Getting in Car
I need yet another reminder, I'm afraid.
Today

FIGURE 12-12: Select Hide to hide completed reminders in macOS.

To mark reminders as complete in iCloud.com:

1. **In the left sidebar, select a list to see its reminders.**
2. **Select the circle next to a reminder to mark it complete.**

   The reminder disappears, but it's not deleted.

3. **To see or hide the completed reminders, click the three blue dots icon in the upper right, and then select Show Completed (see Figure 12-13) or Hide Completed to toggle between the two.**

   You can't delete reminders in iCloud.com.

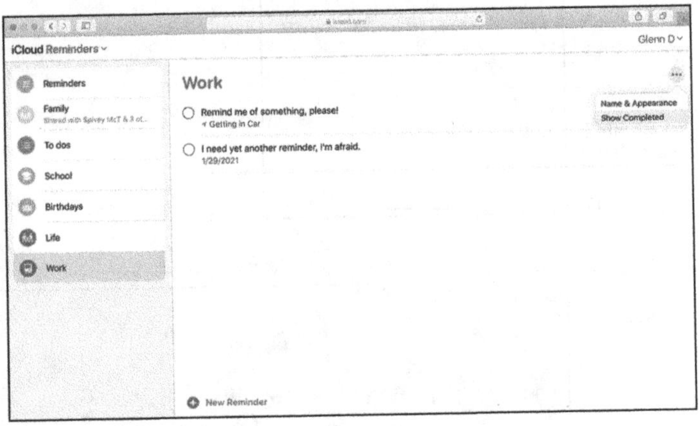
iCloud Reminders
Glenn D
Reminders
Family
To dos
School
Birthdays
Life
Work
Work
Remind me of something, please!
Getting in Car
I need yet another reminder, I'm afraid.
1/29/2021
Name & Appearance
Show Completed
New Reminder

FIGURE 12-13: Show or hide completed reminders in iCloud.com.

In this chapter you discovered how to keep on top of your days, weeks, and months. Sorry, but you don't have any more excuses for not getting the honey-do's done!

» Create and work in notes

» Add, edit, and organize contacts

Chapter 13
Noting Notes and Contacting Contacts

Most of us have had ideas that we just knew were going to change the world for the better and would etch our name in the history books for all time — and then we forget them. Or we come up with some nifty new recipe on the fly, only to — you guessed it — forget the idea that would have cemented our legacy on Food Network.

Notes to the rescue! Once again, Apple have assigned a title to an app that describes it to a tee; Notes helps you take notes. Those notes can be one word or a full-fledged manuscript for the next Oscar winner. You can even use Notes to scan paper documents, such as letters and receipts, for safekeeping.

Contacts is another handy-dandy (to borrow an adjective from my trusty editor, Susan) tool with a name that screams out the reason for its existence: creating, editing, and organizing your contacts. Add phone numbers, nicknames, locations, and even birthdays — no more excuses to miss one!

Note to Self

Notes is a note-taking app introduced to the world with the first iPhone way back in 2007. Since those early days, it has evolved into an indispensable tool for many Apple users and is now available in iOS, iPadOS, macOS, and iCloud.com. Notes are synchronized almost effortlessly using your Apple ID; of course, you'll need to be signed in with your Apple ID on every device that you want to sync your notes with. Any notes you create or edit on one device will automatically appear and sync with another.

Access Notes

In this section, you discover how to enable, access, and synchronize Notes on your devices. One thing to remember: You'll need to be signed in to your Apple ID on whatever devices you want to sync notes with: any combination of iPhone, iPad, and Mac. (If you need a refresher, refer to Chapter 8.)

Windows, Linux, and Android users can access Notes only via a web browser through iCloud.com.

iCloud.com

All Apple One subscribers can access their notes with the iCloud.com website's Notes app:

1. **Open a web browser and go to `www.icloud.com`.**
2. **Enter your Apple ID and password when prompted.**
3. **Click Notes to launch the web version of Notes.**

Apple devices

To sync notes with your Apple devices, you must ensure that Notes is enabled on them. To enable syncing and open the Notes app on your iPhone or iPad:

1. **Open the Settings app.**
2. **Tap your Apple ID at the top of the Settings list.**

3. **Tap iCloud.**
4. **Tap the Notes switch to enable it (if it's not already enabled).**
5. **Leave the Settings app.**

   To do so on an iPhone or iPad that uses Face ID, swipe up. On an iPhone or iPad with a Home button, press Home.

6. **Tap to open the Notes app and your notes will be there.**

To enable and access Notes on your Mac:

1. **Click in the top-left corner and select System Preferences.**
2. **Select Apple ID.**
3. **Select the box next to Notes to enable it, if it's not already selected.**
4. **Open your Applications folder.**
5. **Double-click the Notes app icon to open it.**

Working with Notes

The Notes app looks and behaves nearly the same regardless of which device or platform you use to access it. You can perform most of the same functions in almost the same manner whether using an iPhone, an iPad, or a Mac, and many of the functions are also available in iCloud.com. Since Notes for iCloud works so similarly to Notes on Apple devices, I cover a few basics and then tackle a few additional tasks that can be performed only in the Notes app in iOS, iPad OS, and macOS.

The lay of the land

The keys to getting started using just about any new app, especially one that is used slightly differently on various devices and platforms, are to learn how to get around in it and to understand which tools are at your disposal. Let's check out Notes and see how it looks on your devices.

iCloud.COM

Notes for iCloud is simple to navigate and master, with enough basic tools to get the job done. Figure 13-1 is a map to the Notes for iCloud interface.

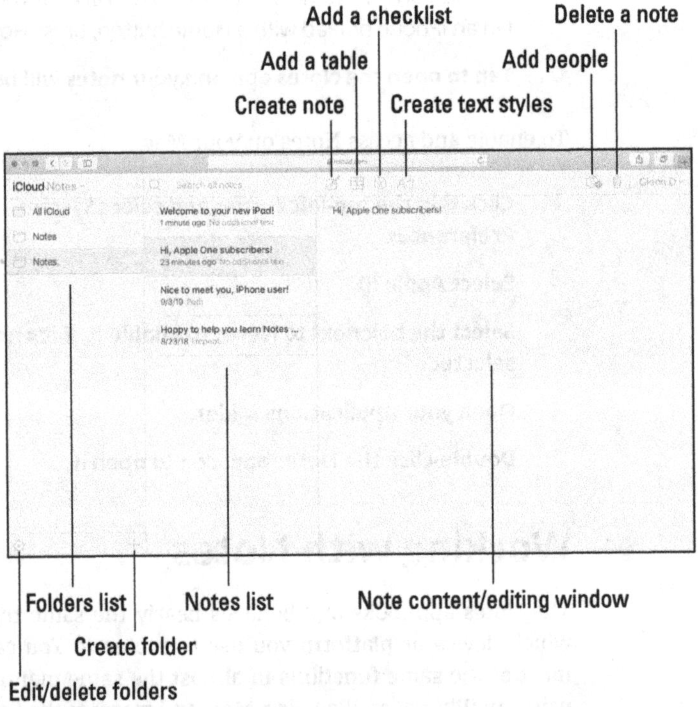
Add a checklist
Delete a note
Add a table
Add people
Create note
Create text styles
Folders list
Notes list
Note content/editing window
Create folder
Edit/delete folders

FIGURE 13-1: Notes for iCloud is super user friendly.

Most options are self-explanatory, but some deserve a bit more discussion:

- **Create text styles:** Click to format your text with bold, italics, underlines, or strikethroughs. You can use this tool also to add numbered and bulleted lists.
- **Add people:** Click to invite others to view or edit your note. You can either email them or share a link to the note. A participant must have an Apple ID to edit and view a note.

Locked notes cannot be shared.

macOS

Notes for macOS looks similar to Notes for iCloud, with several additional tools for you to gussy up your notes. Figure 13-2 is your Notes for macOS guide.

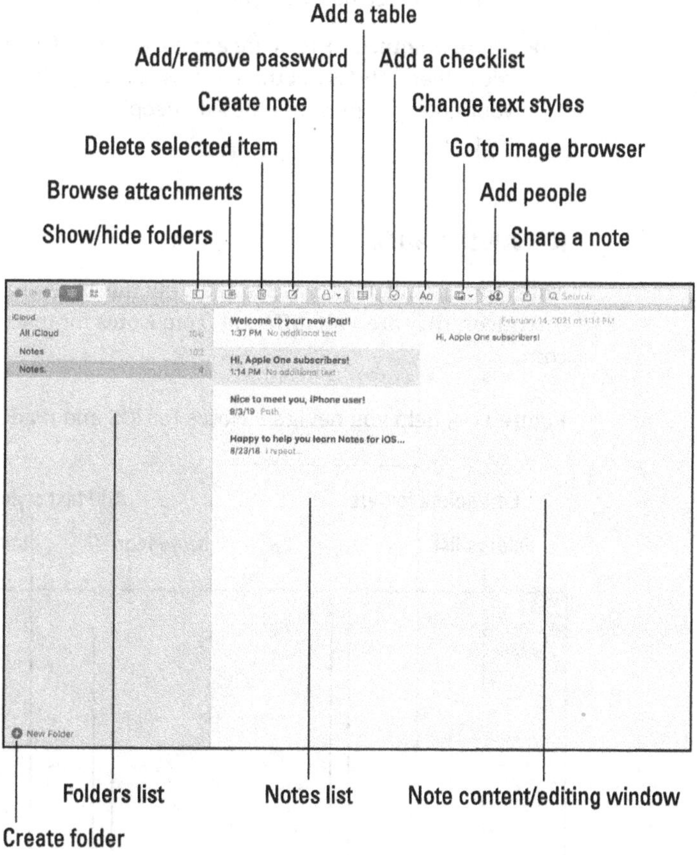
Add a table
Add/remove password
Add a checklist
Create note
Change text styles
Delete selected item
Go to image browser
Browse attachments
Add people
Show/hide folders
Share a note
Folders list
Notes list
Note content/editing window
Create folder

FIGURE 13-2: Notes for macOS is similar to Notes for iCloud, but with more bells and whistles.

Most options don't need explanation, but the following do. Note that some were explained in the preceding section:

- **Browse attachments:** Click to search your notes for attachments you've added to them. For example, you can use this feature to find a note to which you attached a scan of a receipt.

» **Add/remove password:** Click to add a password to a selected note or folder. This helps secure your notes from prying eyes.

» **Go to image browser:** Click to add images from your Mac or a nearby iPhone or iPad to your note. You can also add scans and sketches from your iPhone or iPad.

» **Share a note:** Click to share a static version of your note with others. This is not the same as allowing others to edit your note; you must use the Add People tool to accomplish that.

iOS AND iPadOS

Notes for iOS and iPadOS are similar, but due to the nature of their interfaces, they are a bit different from Notes for macOS or iCloud.com.

Figure 13-3 help you navigate Notes for iOS and iPadOS.

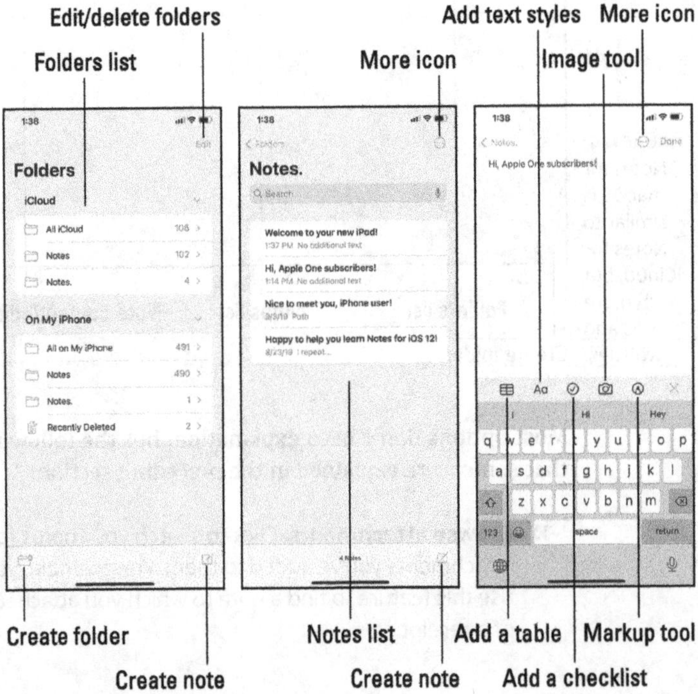

Edit/delete folders
Folders list
More icon
Add text styles
More icon
Image tool
Folders
iCloud
All iCloud
Notes
Notes.
On My iPhone
All on My iPhone
Notes
Notes.
Recently Deleted
Notes.
Welcome to your new iPad!
Hi, Apple One subscribers!
Nice to meet you, iPhone user!
Happy to help you learn Notes for iOS 12!
Hi, Apple One subscribers!
Create folder
Create note
Notes list
Create note
Add a table
Add a checklist
Markup tool

FIGURE 13-3: Notes for iOS and iPadOS is robust.

As with other iterations of the Notes app, most options in iOS and iPadOS don't need an explanation. However, some do need a bit more fleshing out (and some were explained previously section):

» **More icon:** Click to see additional tools, which vary based on which screen you're viewing:
   - If you click the More icon from the list of notes in a folder, you can select, share, add, sort, rename, or move folders, and also see attachments in them.
   - If you click the More icon in a note, you can share it, send a copy of it, move it, and find text in it (particularly useful if the note is lengthy). You may also add a scan, pin the note, lock it, or delete it.

» **Image tool:** Click to add images or videos from your iPhone or iPad to your note. You can also use your iPhone or iPad camera to scan documents and save them in the note.

» **Markup tool:** Click to write or draw on your notes. The Markup tool lets you use your finger or the Apple Pencil (iPad only, if your model supports it) as a pen, pencil, or marker to make comments and add personalized touches.

Visit Apple's Support site to find out which Apple Pencil version is supported for your iPad: `https://support.apple.com/en-us/HT211029`.

Scan documents

If you're like me, you have difficulty hanging on to paper documents such as receipts, lists, and notes. Apple has helped solve that problem by enabling you to use your iPhone or iPad camera to scan paper documents using the Notes app.

You may be wondering why you shouldn't just take a picture of the paper doc and be done with it. Pictures are typically in color, so taking one of a black-and-white receipt just makes for an unnecessarily large file, bytes-wise. Scanning the file in black and white prevents files from being too large, and also helps keep text clear and legible.

To scan paper documents with your iPhone or iPad:

1. **Tap the Image tool (refer to Figure 13-3) and tap Scan Documents to engage the camera.**
2. **Place the document you want to scan on a dark background and center it on the screen using your camera.**

   If the document is centered properly, your camera will automatically take a picture or scan. If not, tap the white button. Continue the process if you want to add multiple pages to the scan.
3. **Tap the Save button in the lower-right corner to add the scan to your note and close the camera.**
4. **Tap the scan in your note if you'd like to edit it.**

   From here you can add more pages to the scan, crop it, select color, grayscale, or black and white for its format (shown in Figure 13-4), rotate it, or delete it.

4:02
Done
Retake
Go SAC
Badgers!
Color
Grayscale
Black & White
Photo
Crop
Rotate
Color format
Delete

FIGURE 13-4: Select a color format for your scan; black and white is best for text.

5. **Tap Done at the top of the screen when finished editing your scan.**

3 . . . 2 . . . 1 . . . Contact!

Back in the day, we used to use a Rolodex, a notebook, or the infamous "little black book" to keep lists of contacts. Phone numbers, addresses, and other assorted information about our neighbors, family, acquaintances, and exterminators were easily found in those pages. But today, many rely on electronic versions of these icons, and for us Apple fans, Contacts is the tool that comes with our devices.

Access Contacts

You want your contacts to be available across all your devices. Let's see how to enable, access, and synchronize Contacts.

You need to be signed into your Apple ID on the devices with which you want to sync contacts. Refer to Chapter 8 for help with that process.

Windows, Linux, and Android users can access Contacts only via their favorite web browser through iCloud.com.

iCloud.com

The iCloud.com Contacts app is the universal way for all to gain access, regardless of their computing platform of choice:

1. **Open a web browser and go to `www.icloud.com`.**
2. **Enter your Apple ID and password when prompted.**
3. **Click the Contents button to launch the web app.**

Apple devices

To keep contacts synchronized devices, you must make sure Contacts is enabled on them. To enable syncing and open the Contacts app on your iPhone or iPad:

1. **Open the Settings app.**
2. **Tap your Apple ID at the top of the Settings list.**
3. **Tap iCloud.**
4. **Tap the Contacts switch to enable it (if it's not already enabled).**
5. **Leave the Settings app.**

   If your iPhone or iPad uses Face ID, swipe up to leave Settings. If your iPhone or iPad has a Home button, press it to leave Settings.
6. **Tap to open the Contacts app and see your contacts.**

To enable and access Contacts on your Mac:

1. **Click in the top-left corner and select System Preferences.**
2. **Select Apple ID.**
3. **Select the box next to Contacts to enable it, if it's not already selected.**
4. **Open your Applications folder.**
5. **Double-click the Contacts app icon to open it.**

Working with Contacts

Like Notes, Contact looks and behaves much the same, no matter the device or platform you use it with. Let's see how to use Contacts in iCloud, iOS, iPad OS, and macOS.

Knowing your way around

Contacts is organized by cards and groups (in the form of folders). Cards hold the information for your contacts, much like cards in a Rolodex, and groups help you keep your cards in easy-to-find spots.

iCloud.COM

Contacts for iCloud is easy-peasy to move around and work in, providing most of the tools available in its cousin apps on iOS, iPadOS, and macOS.

Figure 13-5 shows you the layout of Contacts when viewed in iCloud.com, which can be accessed from any Internet-connected device on the planet.

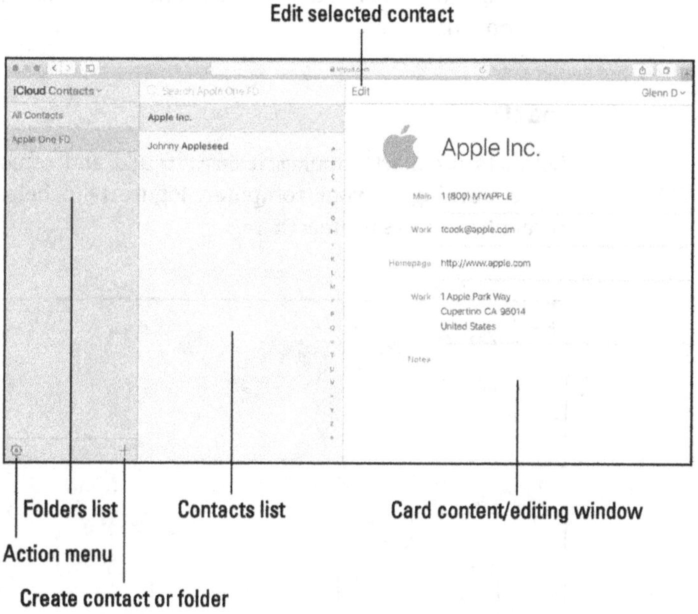

Edit selected contact
iCloud Contacts
All Contacts
Apple Inc.
Johnny Appleseed
Edit
Glenn D
Apple Inc.
Folders list
Contacts list
Card content/editing window
Action menu
Create contact or folder

FIGURE 13-5: The Contacts app in iCloud makes it easy to find anyone from anywhere.

Let's take a slightly longer look at some of the available options and features:

- **Action menu:** Click this icon to adjust preferences, import and export virtual cards (vCards), delete contacts, and more. Preferences allows you to select a default sorting method for your contacts, as well as a default address format based on a particular country.

  vCards are digital files containing contact information. You can share vCards with others, whether they use Contacts, a third-party contacts app, or even a contacts app on a different platform (such as Microsoft Outlook for Windows).

» **Edit selected contact:** Select an existing contact, and then click the Edit button to edit their information. I won't leave you hanging.

Here are some of the options available when editing a contact's info in Contacts for iCloud: name and company; picture; phone numbers and email addresses; web page URL; home and company street addresses; notes related to the contact (such as favorite color or restaurant). You can also add a field if the one you want isn't available. Click the blue Add Field button and select one of the available options.

macOS

Contacts for macOS makes it easy to add and remove contacts while working on your computer. Figure 13-6 helps guide you through Contacts for macOS.

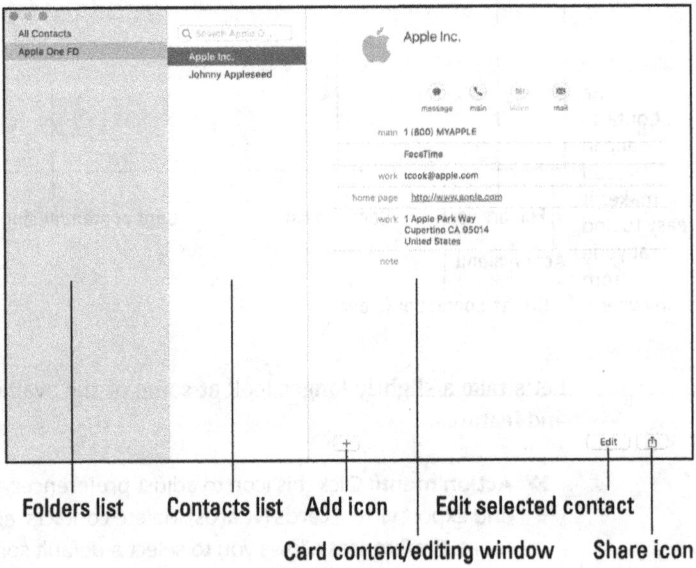
All Contacts
Apple One FD
Apple Inc.
Johnny Appleseed
Apple Inc.
main 1 (800) MYAPPLE
FaceTime
work tcook@apple.com
home page http://www.apple.com
work 1 Apple Park Way
Cupertino CA 95014
United States
note
Edit
Folders list
Contacts list
Add icon
Edit selected contact
Card content/editing window
Share icon

FIGURE 13-6: Contacts is a breeze to use in macOS.

Let's take a peek at some features that need a tad bit of explanation:

- **Add icon:** Click to create a new contact, new group, or to add additional fields to the currently selected contact.
- **Share icon:** Click to share the currently selected contact. This option allows you to send a vCard for the contact via other apps on your Mac, such as Mail or Messages.

iOS AND iPadOS

Again, like Notes, Contacts for iOS and iPadOS are similar to each other but, due to the kinds of devices they run on, a little different from Contacts for macOS or iCloud.com.

Figure 13-7 will get you from place to place in Contacts for iOS and iPadOS.

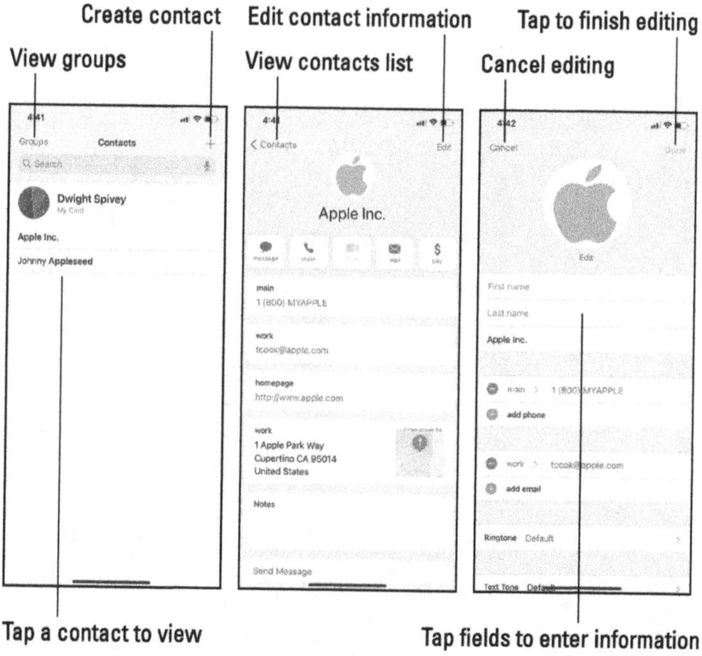
Create contact
Edit contact information
Tap to finish editing
View groups
View contacts list
Cancel editing
Groups
Contacts
Dwight Spivey
Apple Inc.
Johnny Appleseed
Apple Inc.
Edit
Cancel
Tap a contact to view
Tap fields to enter information

FIGURE 13-7: Contacts allows you to add all sorts of good information about your contacts.

Apple makes things so intuitive that most of these options can be understood easily without much fanfare. Others have been touched on earlier in the chapter.

Scroll down a bit in the editing window if you'd like to add a field that's not already there by default. Tap the blue Add Field button, select a listed option, and then enter the required info.

TIP

Although it's important to maintain contact records for others, it's also a good idea to keep your own contact record up-to-date.

This tour of Notes and Contacts should help you get started keeping your thoughts and contact info neat and tidy. Find out more about both by visiting Apple's Support site at `https://support.apple.com`; just click the Search field and type your topic or question.

IN THIS CHAPTER

» Accessing your apps

» Producing beautiful documents with Pages

» Crunching numbers with Numbers spreadsheets

» Introducing Keynote presentations

Chapter 14

Docs and Spreadsheets and Presentations, Oh My!

Most folks on the planet have heard of Microsoft's venerable set of applications typically known as Office. Office includes Word for word processing and page layout, Excel for spreadsheets and charts, and PowerPoint for creating and delivering presentations, among other apps. Whether you work in a high-rise building, a classroom, or on your back porch, chances are you've used one or all of them at some point in your life.

Well, Apple has a similar set of tools that provide the same services, but with the benefits of being more user-friendly and accessible than their more famous Microsoft counterparts. Pages, Numbers, and Keynote were introduced as part of Apple's iWork suite of productivity tools back in 2005. Pages handles word processing and page layout (similar to MS Word), Numbers is a spreadsheet tool (like Excel), and Keynote is Apple's equivalent to PowerPoint.

In this chapter, you learn how to access each of these tools, and get a good head start on using them across your devices.

Accessing and Working with iWork Apps

Pages, Numbers, and Keynote are preinstalled on every Apple smart device and computer: iPhones, iPads, and Macs. However, the apps look slightly different and some options may be found in different locations, depending on which device you're using them on.

Figure 14-1 illustrates the differences in appearance between Pages for Mac, iOS, and iCloud.com.

TODAY'S NEWS
TODAY'S NEWS
5:32
TODAY'S NEWS

FIGURE 14-1: Same app, different look, depending on how you access it.

TIP

If you can't find the apps on your Mac, iPhone, or iPad, visit the App Store on your device, search for the missing app(s), and download them. They're free for all to download and use.

Some features may be limited in the iCloud.com version of the iWork apps. For example, you can't upload videos or audio files into Pages documents using iCloud.com, so you must use the Pages app on your Mac, iPhone, or iPad to do so.

TIP

Apple's Support site has more information regarding the feature differences and limitations of the iWork apps on iCloud.com: `https://support.apple.com/en-us/HT202690`.

When using a Mac, you can find the apps in your Applications folder. If using an iPhone or iPad, the apps are in one of your Home screens. The iCloud.com versions can be accessed from most Internet-capable computers, which is the only way Windows and Linux users can take advantage of Pages, Numbers, and Keynote. Unfortunately, Android users can't utilize these apps in iCloud.com: They don't even appear as options.

To get to the apps via iCloud.com:

1. **Open your favorite web browser on you Mac, iPhone, iPad, or PC (running Windows or Linux).**
2. **Go to `www.icloud.com` and log in with your Apple ID username and password.**
3. **Click the icon for Pages, Numbers, or Keynote to open the app.**

As with everything else iCloud-related, your Apple ID keeps everything synced so that whatever items you create on one device are almost instantly available on another. You sign in with your Apple ID on every device that you want to use with iWork apps. For example, if you edit a spreadsheet in Numbers using iCloud.com, those edits immediately (or close to it) appear in Numbers on your iPad, as long as both are signed in to the same Apple ID.

REMEMBER

Please note that these apps work similarly to one another, regardless of the hardware and software platform they're accessed from. Having said that, because this section of the book is focused on iCloud.com and I don't have room to cover every aspect of the iWork suite across all platforms, I keep the focus on working with the iCloud.com version of these apps.

Using and Saving Files

Each of the three iWork apps supports a wide range of file types, even allowing the import and export of some Microsoft Office files and PDFs. This info is super important when working with others who may not have Pages, Numbers, or Keynote. You can also save files to your device or to your iCloud Drive.

Supported file types

Each of the apps can open files and convert files based on the type of documents they're designed to use.

Pages

Pages on all platforms can open Pages files of all versions, Microsoft Word files (.docx and .doc), Rich Text Format (.rtf and .rtfd), and Plain Text files (.txt).

Pages for iCloud.com can convert files to Microsoft Word (.docx only), PDF, and EPUB (used for electronic books). Pages for iOS and iPadOS can convert to those same file types, as well as Rich Text Format (.rtf). Finally, Pages for Mac can convert to all these file types, as well as Microsoft Word (.docx and .doc), Plain Text (.txt), and Pages '09.

Numbers

Numbers on all platforms can open Numbers files of all versions, Microsoft Excel (.xlsx and .xls), comma-separated values (.csv), and tab-delimited or fixed-width text files.

Numbers for iCloud.com can convert files to Microsoft Excel (.xlsx only), PDF, and comma-separated values (.csv). Numbers for iOS and iPadOS can convert to these same file types, as well as tab-separated values (.tsv). Numbers for Mac can convert to all these file types, as well as Microsoft Excel (.xlsx and .xls) and Numbers '09.

Keynote

Keynote on all platforms can open Keynote files of all versions and Microsoft PowerPoint (.pptx and .ppt) files.

Keynote for iCloud.com can export files to Microsoft PowerPoint (.pptx only) and PDF. Keynote for iOS and iPadOS can convert to these same file types, as well as movie (.mov), images (.jpeg, .png, or .tiff), and animated GIF types. Keynote for Mac can convert to all these file types, as well as Microsoft Word (.pptx and .ppt), movie (.m4v or .mov), HTML, and Keynote '09.

WARNING

Please be aware that the formatting of text and images may change when working with converted files. For example, if you convert a Pages document to Microsoft Word and then try to open the converted file with Word on a PC, the text may appear differently if the font used in the original document isn't installed on the PC. Another example is that you might find extra spaces in the sentences of converted files.

Saving files

Pages, Numbers, and Keynote can save files to your Mac, iPhone, iPad, or PC. They can also save files to your iCloud Drive, which is the only way to open the same file on several or all of your devices. For example, if you save a file in iCloud Drive from Numbers on your Mac, you can open it in the Numbers app on your iPad while you're waiting for your ride.

For more information on iCloud Drive, including how to save files to it and open files from it, see Chapter 9.

Creating and Editing Pages Docs in iCloud

Pages lets you create documents from the most basic of text files to elaborate and lovely brochures and newsletters, and much more in between. It's a word processor and a page layout application rolled into one.

Pages in iCloud.com is surprisingly powerful and versatile for a web-based app, but simple enough that its layout is still clean and useful in most modern web browsers.

Managing documents

When you first access Pages in iCloud.com, you're presented with the document manager, which allows you to — wait for it — manage your documents. From here (refer to Figure 14-2) you can see documents you've recently worked in, browse for documents in iCloud Drive, view shared documents, and check out files you've recently deleted.

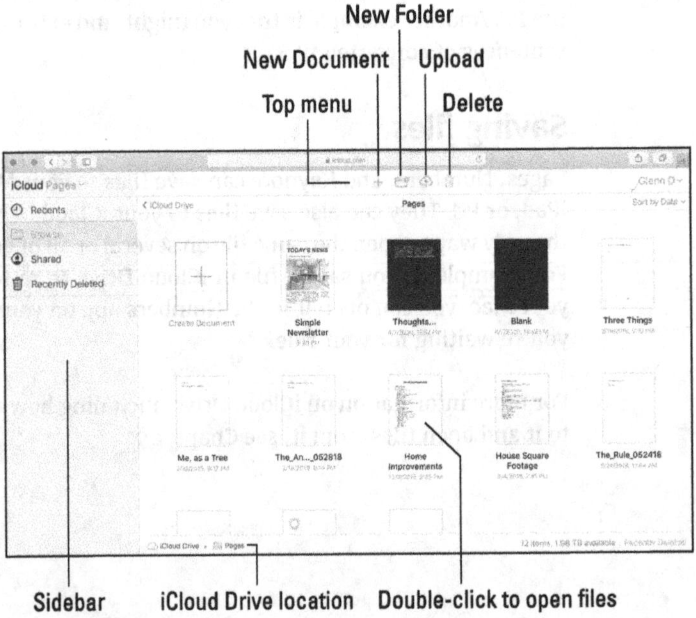

New Folder
New Document
Upload
Top menu
Delete
Sidebar
iCloud Drive location
Double-click to open files

FIGURE 14-2: The document manager is where you'll find your Pages documents.

WARNING

Deleted files remain in iCloud Drive for only 30 days, after which they're sent packing for good.

The document manager also allows you to do the following:

- **Create documents in iCloud Drive.** Click (Mac or PC) or tap (iPhone or iPad) the + icon at the top of the window to open a new document in a new tab or window in your browser. Select a template from the list and get going.
- **Create folders in iCloud Drive to stay organized.** Click or tap the new folder icon (labeled in Figure 14-2) at the top of the window, and then give the new folder a descriptive name.
- **Upload documents from your computer, iPhone, or iPad to iCloud Drive.** Click or tap the upload icon at the top of the window, select a file that's stored on your device, then click or tap Choose, Open, or whatever your browser calls the button you need to click or tap to proceed.
- **Delete documents in iCloud Drive.** Click or tap to select an item in the document manager, and then click or tap the delete icon (trash can) at the top of the window.

Working in documents

After you've created a document, it's time to add content and perhaps spruce it up a bit (or a lot). Figure 14-3 gives you the document viewer's lay of the land to help you find the most important tools when working with a Pages document.

Although some of the icons labeled in Figure 14-3 are self-explanatory, others need a bit of teasing out:

- **Show/hide:** Several tools, such as a ruler and a word count, are hidden from view, but you can show or hide them using the show/hide icon in the upper left of the screen.
- **Insert page elements:** Click or tap this icon to insert breaks, page numbers, and footnotes.

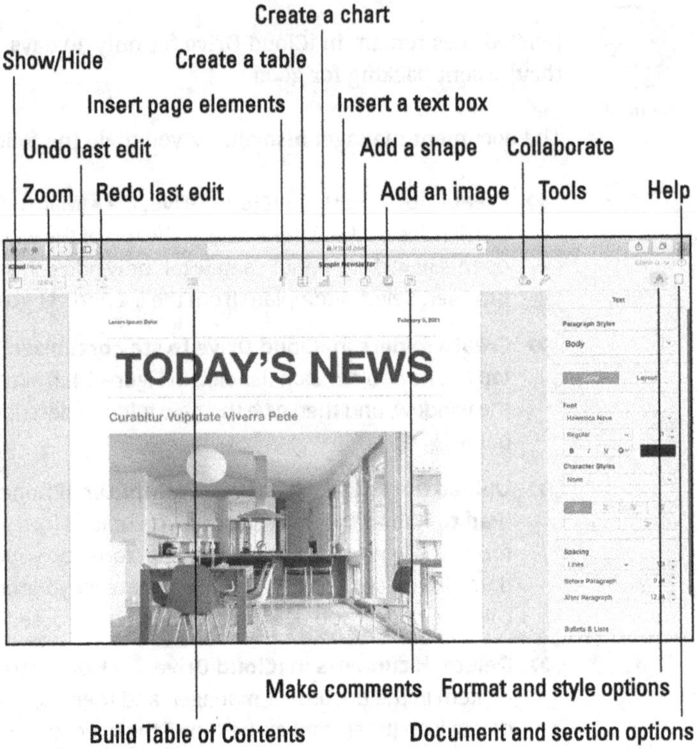
Create a chart
Show/Hide
Create a table
Insert page elements
Insert a text box
Undo last edit
Add a shape
Collaborate
Zoom
Redo last edit
Add an image
Tools
Help
TODAY'S NEWS
Curabitur Vulputate Viverra Pede
Make comments
Format and style options
Build Table of Contents
Document and section options

FIGURE 14-3: The document viewer is where the magic happens!

- **Collaborate:** Click or tap the collaborate icon to share your document via email invitation or by getting a link for the document. You can share and collaborate with others, even if they don't typically use iCloud. Note that some sharing and collaboration requires signing in with an Apple ID.

  TIP

  Look at the "Share and Collaborate" section of the *Pages User Guide for iCloud* for all the details regarding sharing and collaboration: `https://support.apple.com/guide/pages-icloud/welcome/icloud`.

- **Tools:** Click or tap the wrench icon to access several tools at your disposal:
  - *Download a Copy:* Download a copy of your document as a Pages, PDF, Word, or EPUB file.
  - *Send a Copy:* Email a copy of your document as a Pages, PDF, Word, or EPUB file.
  - *Print:* Print a PDF of your document, which opens in a new browser tab.

- *Browse All Versions:* Pages for iCloud automatically saves versions of your file, allowing you to revert to previous versions if you accidentally wreak havoc upon the document.
- *Go to My Documents:* Go to Document Manager.
- *Set Password:* Create a password for access to this document.
- *Preferences:* Customize commenting options and utilize alignment guides, which help you center content.
- *Publish to Apple Books*: Publish your document as an Apple Book.

TIP

Check out the "Publish to Apple Books" section of the *Pages User Guide for iCloud* to learn how to publish your document as a book in Apple's digital book platform: `https://support.apple.com/guide/pages-icloud/welcome/icloud`.

» **Format and style options:** These options help you customize fonts, sentence spacing, bullets and lists, and much more. The available options will differ depending on whether you selected text or an image in the document.

» **Document and section options:** Edit and customize items such as page size, page orientation, page numbers, and more.

» **Help:** This option speaks for itself, but I wanted to highlight it because I don't have the space to explain all the bells and whistles of Pages. Click or tap the help icon (question mark) to gain access to loads of information from Apple regarding all things Pages for iCloud.

Working with Spreadsheets in Numbers

Spreadsheets are as necessary to run a business (and some homes) as wind is to push a sailboat. I've used spreadsheets since the early 1990s, and there is no love lost between us. They're usually ugly and boring, and tools in most spreadsheet applications are confusing and unintuitive. I will say that in recent years Microsoft has stepped up their game and made crucial functional and aesthetic improvements, but when it comes to making things easier and more visually appealing, few software developers can compete with Apple. Don't get me wrong; Microsoft Excel is the best overall tool for folks who have to deal with heavy-duty industrial-sized spreadsheets, but Apple's Numbers works incredibly well for the rest of us. And it looks darned good doing it, too.

Managing spreadsheets

The default screen in Numbers in iCloud.com is the spreadsheet manager, shown in Figure 14-4. The spreadsheet manager displays your recent spreadsheets, and enables you to view spreadsheets stored in iCloud Drive, access shared documents, and see spreadsheets you've recently deleted.

The spreadsheet manager helps you to do the following:

- **Create spreadsheets in iCloud Drive.** Click (Mac or PC) or tap (iPhone or iPad) the + icon at the top of the window or in the Browse window to open a new spreadsheet in a new tab or window in your browser. Select a template from the list provided and start spreadsheeting.
- **Create folders in iCloud Drive to keep your spreadsheets organized.** Click or tap the new folder icon (labeled in Figure 14-4) at the top of the window, and then give the new folder a descriptive name.
- **Upload spreadsheets from your computer, iPhone, or iPad to iCloud Drive.** Click or tap the upload icon at the top of the window, select a spreadsheet that's stored on your device, and then click or tap Choose, Open, or whatever your browser calls the button you need to click or tap to proceed.
- **Delete spreadsheets in iCloud Drive.** Click or tap to select a spreadsheet in Spreadsheet Manager, and then click or tap the delete icon (trash can) at the top of the window.

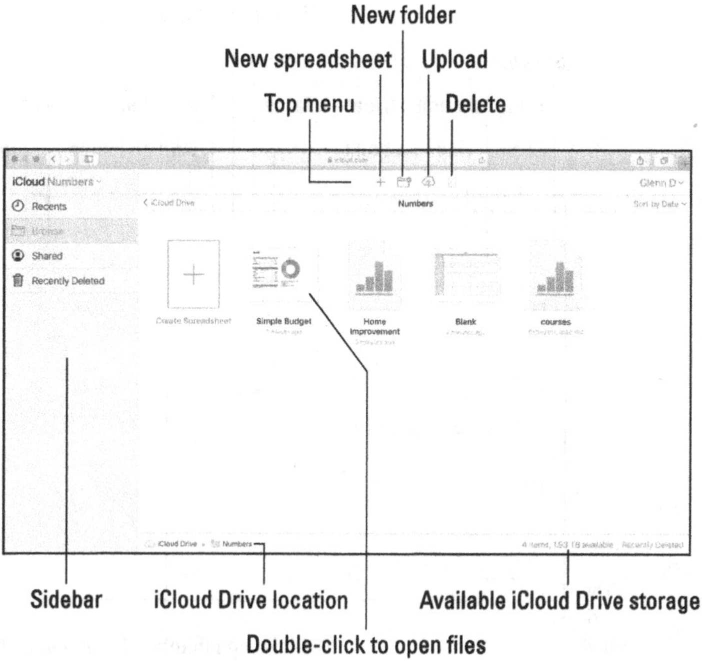
New folder
New spreadsheet
Upload
Top menu
Delete
iCloud Numbers
Recents
Shared
Recently Deleted
Numbers
Simple Budget
Home Improvement
Blank
courses
Sidebar
iCloud Drive location
Available iCloud Drive storage
Double-click to open files

FIGURE 14-4: The spreadsheet manager managing spreadsheets.

Working in spreadsheets

Spreadsheets don't do much good if you don't populate them with data and graphics, so learning your way around the Numbers landscape is essential. The spreadsheet viewer is where the real work's done.

Figure 14-5 shows you the most important tools at your disposal when working in a spreadsheet in Numbers for iCloud.

As with the document viewer in Pages, the spreadsheet viewer contains some options that don't need much explanation, but others do require a bit:

» **Show/hide:** Show or hide the Find & Replace tool or comments by clicking the show/hide icon. (All icons are labeled in Figure 14-5.)

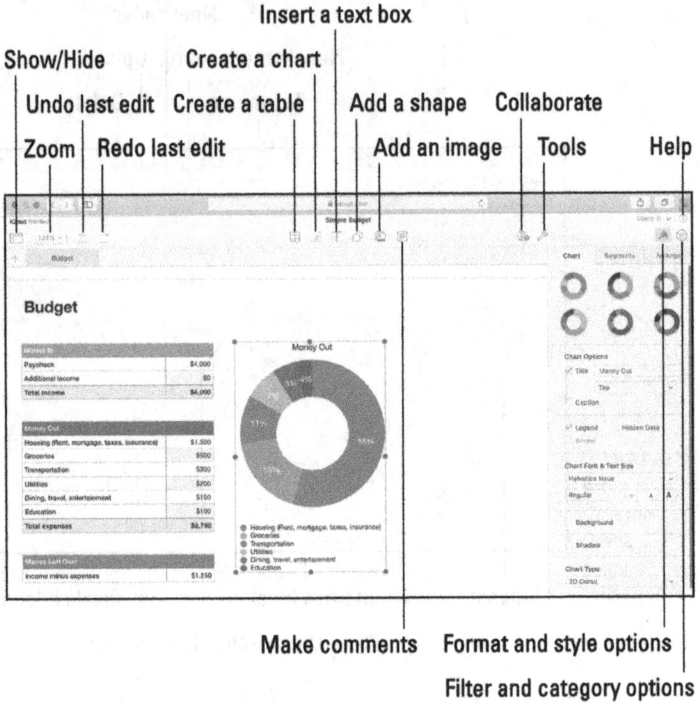
Insert a text box
Show/Hide
Create a chart
Undo last edit
Create a table
Add a shape
Collaborate
Zoom
Redo last edit
Add an image
Tools
Help
Budget
Money Out
Make comments
Format and style options
Filter and category options

FIGURE 14-5: The spreadsheet viewer in all its glory.

- **Collaborate:** Click or tap the collaborate icon to share your spreadsheet. I highly suggest taking a look at the "Share and Collaborate" section of the *Numbers User Guide for iCloud* for help figuring out the options available: `https://support.apple.com/guide/numbers-icloud/welcome/icloud`.
- **Tools:** Click or tap the tools icon (wrench) to utilize the following tools:
  - *Download a Copy:* Download a copy of your spreadsheet as a Numbers, PDF, Excel, or CSV file.
  - *Send a Copy:* Email a copy of your spreadsheet as a Numbers, PDF, Excel, or CSV file.
  - *Print:* Print a PDF of your spreadsheet, which appears in a new browser tab.
  - *Browse All Versions:* Numbers saves versions of your file as you make changes so you can revert to previous versions if you desired (or it is necessary).

- *Go to My Spreadsheets:* Go to the spreadsheet manager.
- *Set Password:* Secure your spreadsheet with a password to offer another layer of protection for your sensitive info.
- *Preferences:* Customize commenting options and use alignment guides to help you center content.

» **Format and style options:** These options help you customize fonts, chart types, table colors, and data formats; group and ungroup items; and tons more.

» **Filter and category options:** Group spreadsheet rows into categories for organization and create filters to help you quickly sift through mountains of information for the data you need.

» **Help:** Tap Help to open the *Numbers User Guide for iCloud,* which provides much more information than I can squeeze into this chapter.

TIP

You can access the *Numbers User Guide for iCloud* also on Apple's Support site at `https://support.apple.com/guide/numbers-icloud/welcome/icloud`.

Creating Presentations in Keynote

I don't know that I've ever seen a better presenter, in-person or otherwise, than Steve Jobs. His messages came across clearly, were concise but informative, and were artfully delivered with an entertainer's flair. In the mid-1990s he would use a presentation software called Concurrence (I doubt he'd ever be caught using PowerPoint) but it wasn't quite what he wanted. And so, Keynote was born.

Keynote has since morphed from Steve Jobs's personal use into a full-fledged presentation software used by throngs of Apple customers, and it can stand toe-to-toe with its competition.

Managing presentations

As with Pages and Numbers, a manager — in this case, the presentation manager — is what you're greeted with when you first launch Keynote in iCloud. As shown in Figure 14-6, you can see recent presentations, browse for presentations in iCloud Drive, see shared presentations, or look for presentations you've deleted in the last 30 days.

The presentation manager is where you can do the following:

- **Create presentations in iCloud Drive.** Click (Mac or PC) or tap (iPhone or iPad) the + icon at the top of the window to open a new presentation in a new tab or window in your browser. Choose one of the prebuilt templates to get started.
- **Organize presentations by creating folders for them.** Click or tap the new folder icon (labeled in Figure 14-6) at the top of the window to create a folder, and then give it a descriptive name.

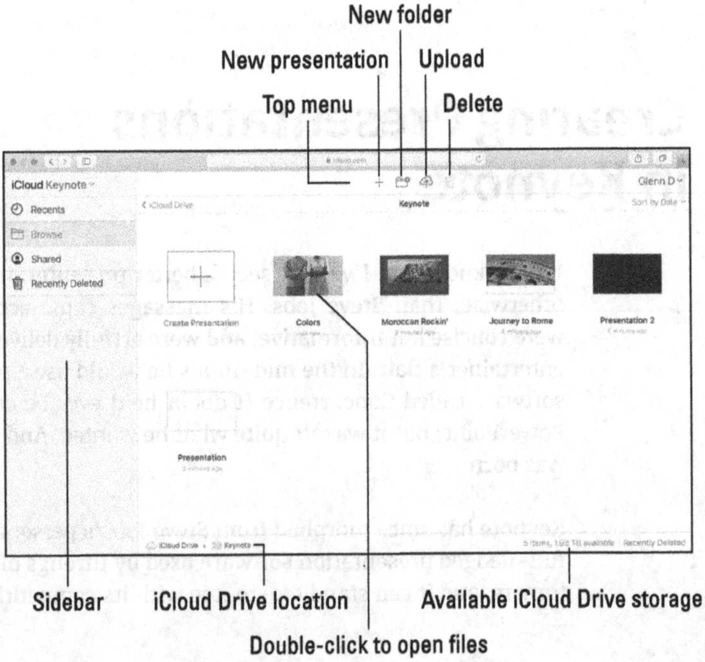
New folder
New presentation
Upload
Top menu
Delete
iCloud Keynote
Recents
Browse
Shared
Recently Deleted
Keynote
Glenn D
Create Presentation
Colors
Moroccan Rockin'
Journey to Rome
Presentation 2
Presentation
Sidebar
iCloud Drive location
Available iCloud Drive storage
Double-click to open files

FIGURE 14-6: The presentation manager is ready to get you started in Keynote.

» **Upload presentations from your computer, iPhone, or iPad to iCloud Drive.** Click or tap the upload icon at the top of the window, select a presentation stored on your computer, iPhone, or iPad, and then click or tap Choose, Open, or whatever term your browser uses to begin the upload.

» **Delete presentations in iCloud Drive.** Click or tap to select a presentation in the presentation manager, and then click or tap the delete icon (trash can) at the top of the window.

Working in presentations

When you create a presentation or open an existing one from the presentation manager, the presentation viewer shown in Figure 14-7 appears.

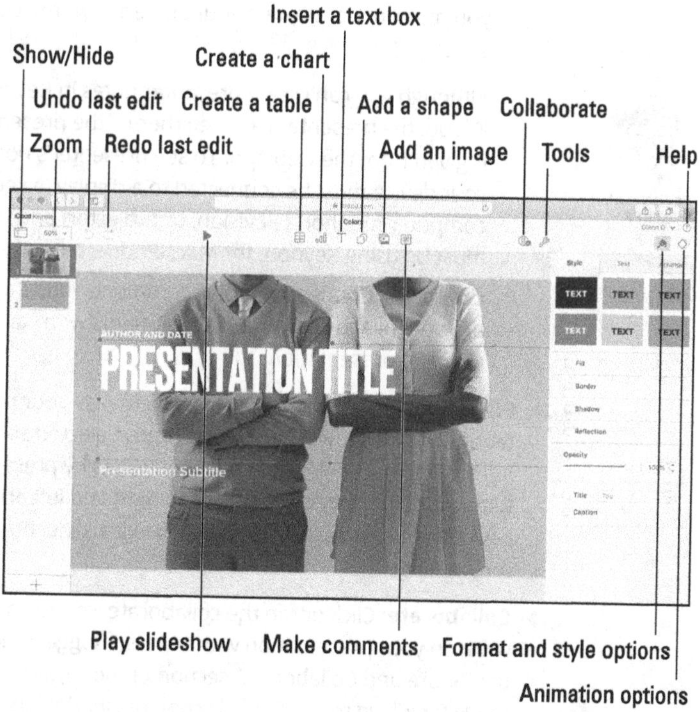
Insert a text box
Show/Hide
Create a chart
Undo last edit
Create a table
Add a shape
Collaborate
Zoom
Redo last edit
Add an image
Tools
Help
AUTHOR AND DATE
PRESENTATION TITLE
Presentation Subtitle
Play slideshow
Make comments
Format and style options
Animation options

FIGURE 14-7: The presentation viewer is ready for action!

TIP

When using presentation viewer in Keynote for iPhone or iPad, you enter reading view by default. To begin editing, just tap the Edit button.

Like the document viewer in Pages and the spreadsheet viewer in Numbers, some of the available tools in the presentation viewer are easy to understand, but a few warrant further brief discussion:

- **Show/hide:** Click the show/hide icon in the far left (labeled in Figure 14-7) to show or hide a few important tools:
  - *Slide Navigator:* Display the slides in your presentation in a sidebar on the left side of the screen. This setting is the default.
  - *Find & Replace:* Quickly find words or phrases and replace them.
  - *Presenter Notes:* View presenter notes, which are visible only to the presenter, to help you recall information that you may not be showing your audience on the current slide.

    TECHNICAL STUFF

    Although you can create presenter notes in Keynote for iCloud, the presenter can't see them if the presentation is given from the web app. To see presenter's notes, your device must be connected to a display (a second computer monitor, television, or projector) and you must be using Keynote for Mac, iPhone, or iPad.
  - *Comments:* Choose to display comments made by you or your collaborators. These comments won't appear during a presentation.
- **Play slideshow:** Click or tap this icon to play your presentation (or slideshow) from the currently selected slide in full-screen mode. Navigate between slides by pressing the Return or Enter key or by using the right and left arrow keys on your keyboard. Press Esc to exit a slideshow before the last slide.
- **Collaborate:** Click or tap the collaborate icon to share and work on your presentation with others. I suggest reading the "Share and Collaborate" section of the *Keynote User Guide for iCloud* to get the full scoop on sharing and

collaboration: `https://support.apple.com/guide/keynote-icloud/welcome/icloud`.

- **Tools:** Click or tap the tools icon (wrench) to access several tools for your presentations:
  - *Use Keynote Live:* This is straight up cool. Keynote Live allows you to give your presentation via the Internet to anyone you want to share it with. The viewers do not need iCloud accounts (which is awesome), but they will need a web browser (for viewing your presentation on any Internet-connected computer or smart device) or the latest version of the Keynote app on their Mac, iPhone, or iPad.

    For help with setting up this great feature, take a gander at the "Play a Presentation" section of the *Keynote User Guide for iCloud* (specifically, the subsection called "On Devices Over the Internet"): `https://support.apple.com/guide/keynote-icloud/welcome/icloud`.
  - *Download a Copy:* Download a copy of your presentation as a Keynote, PDF, or PowerPoint file.
  - *Send a Copy:* Email a copy of your presentation as a Keynote, PDF, or PowerPoint file.
  - *Print:* Print a PDF of your presentation, which appears in a new browser tab.
  - *Browse All Versions:* Keynote for iCloud automatically saves versions of your presentations. Select this option to view them for your presentation and even revert to a previous version.
  - *Go to My Presentations:* Go to Presentation Manager.
  - *Set Password:* Secure your presentation with a password.
  - *Preferences:* Customize commenting options and work with alignment guides to help you center slide content.
- **Format and style options:** These options allow you customize fonts, create bullets and lists, select background colors, and more.

» **Animation options:** You can use animations to make transitions from one slide to the next a tad more interesting. My favorite transition is Magic Move, which animates objects or text that are common from one slide to the next. For example, if you have a word on slide 1 that appears in a different place on slide 2, Magic Move will animate the movement from the word's position in the first slide to the second. It's the little things in life, you know.

» **Help:** Click or tap the help icon (question mark) to be whisked away to the *Keynote User Guide for iCloud* (`https://support.apple.com/guide/keynote-icloud/welcome/10.2/icloud`), which will answer all the questions you have regarding how to make awesome presentations.

This chapter has served to get your feet wet with Pages, Numbers, and Keynote for iCloud. Please dive on into the iWork pool; the water's very fine.

» Locating your devices and friends

Chapter 15
Digital Lost-and-Found

Lost-and-founds have saved my hide on many occasions. I've lost things at schools, jobs, hotels, stores, and airports, only to be graced by the kindness of others who have found and returned my items.

Apple has a digital version of a lost-and-found called Find My. Find My gets its oddly incomplete-sounding name by being a mashup of two previous apps called Find My iPhone and Find My Friends, both of which performed the tasks for which they were aptly named. Find My now performs the functions of both apps.

In this chapter, you learn how to find Apple devices you've misplaced and track down friends you're meeting on your excursions.

REMEMBER

The Find My app is available for and works to find only Apple devices.

Enable and Access Find My

Let's see how to enable and access Find My on your devices. Find My works for your Mac, iPhone, iPad, Apple Watch, and AirPods.

REMEMBER

One important thing to remember: You need to be signed into your Apple ID on whatever devices you want to use with Find My.

iCloud.com

As mentioned, Find My is a combination of two older apps: Find My iPhone and Find My Friends. That holds true except when it comes to iCloud.com; both apps still reside and are used for their respective purposes in iCloud.com (for reasons I've been unable to unearth). To utilize one or both:

1. **Open a web browser and go to `www.icloud.com`.**
2. **Enter your Apple ID and password when prompted.**
3. **Click the Find My iPhone button or the Find My Friends button to launch the web version of either app.**

Apple devices

To use Find My with your Apple devices, you must ensure that Find My is enabled on them. To enable Find My and open its app on your iPhone or iPad:

1. **Open the Settings app.**
2. **Tap your Apple ID at the top of the Settings list.**
3. **Tap Find My, and then tap Find My iPhone or Find My iPad.**
4. **Tap the Find My iPhone or Find My iPad switch to enable it (if it's not already enabled).**

   I also recommend enabling the Find My network option here. This option will help you find your device even when it is offline.

Another option to consider enabling here is Send Last Location, which sends the device's location to Apple when its battery charge begins to wane.

5. **Leave the Settings app.**

   Swipe up on the screen if your iPhone or iPad uses Face ID, or press the Home button if your iPhone or iPad has a Home button.

6. **Tap to open the Find My app.**

To enable and access Find My on your Mac:

1. **Click in the top-left corner of your screen and select System Preferences.**
2. **Select Security & Privacy, and then select the Privacy tab.**

   TIP

   If the padlock in the lower-left of the window is locked, click it, and then enter an administrator's username and password to unlock it.

3. **Select Location Services on the left, and then select the Enable Location Services option.**
4. **Select the Find My option to enable it for your Mac.**
5. **Open your Applications folder.**
6. **Double-click the Find My app icon to open it.**

On the Hunt!

Even if you're someone who's generally great about keeping up with your devices, sometimes life just happens and you need a backup like Find My at your disposal. It's also handy at finding friends if you're meeting them in a crowded or unfamiliar area.

Find My looks and acts a bit differently depending on the device you're using it on. In this section, I give you the tour of the Find My app in all its incarnations to better equip you to find your lost or misplaced Apple toys.

iCloud.com

Remember that the tool for finding lost Apple devices in iCloud.com is still referred to as Find My iPhone (even though it can be used to find your Mac, iPad, Apple Watch, and AirPods, too). Figure 15-1 helps navigate the Find iPhone landscape in iCloud.com.

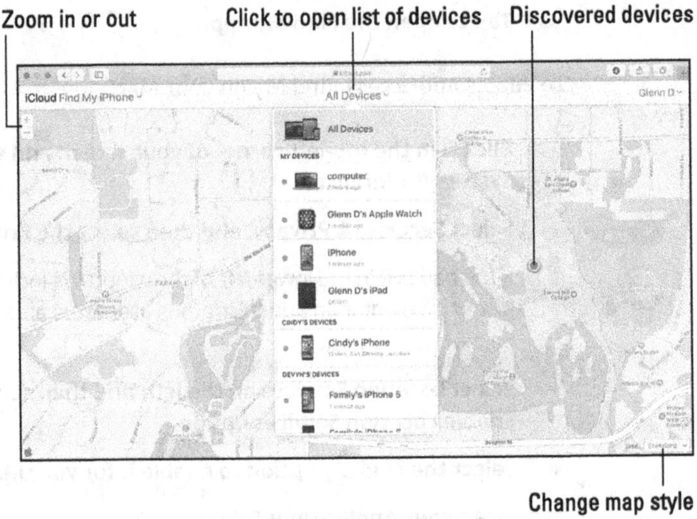
Zoom in or out
Click to open list of devices
Discovered devices
iCloud Find My iPhone
All Devices
All Devices
MY DEVICES
computer
Glenn D's Apple Watch
iPhone
Glenn D's iPad
CINDY'S DEVICES
Cindy's iPhone
Family's iPhone 5
Change map style

FIGURE 15-1: Find iPhone in iCloud.com works with any Internet-connected device's browser.

Found devices are represented on the map by green dots. Click All Devices and select from the list that appears a device for which you want more information. You're then presented with three options for the device:

- **Play Sound:** Click to cause your device to play a loud pinging sound, enabling you to find it more easily if you're within listening range.
- **Lock (Mac) or Lost Mode (iPhone, iPad, and Apple Watch):** Click to lock your device and to disable Apple Pay if it's used on the device. The device can then be unlocked using only your passcode. When you lock or place the device in lost mode, you can add a custom message that will appear on the device's Lock screen.

TIP

It's a good idea to include your phone number or email address so you can be contacted if the device is found by someone else.

- **Erase:** Click to erase the data from your device. This is, of course, the last step you'll want to take, but it will protect your privacy, which is of utmost importance if you believe the device is gone for good or could be in the hands of someone with bad intentions.

WARNING

Erasing your device is a great idea, but it's a last resort! You cannot undo the erasure and you will no longer be able to use Find My to locate the device.

Next stop on the tour of iCloud.com is the Find Friends app. Figure 15-2 shows you the Find My Friends window and its features. They're all self-explanatory. To see a friend's locations, simply click the person's name or device in the Friends list to locate the person on the map. Of course, this is possible only if your friends are indeed sharing their location.

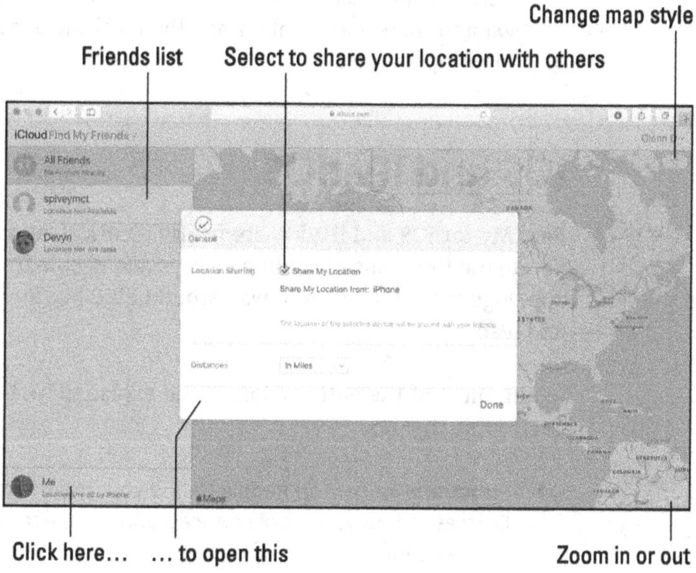

Change map style
Friends list
Select to share your location with others
Click here…
… to open this
Zoom in or out

FIGURE 15-2: Check your friend's location with Find My Friends in iCloud.com.

macOS

Find My on the Mac shares similarities with Find My iPhone for iCloud, but it does have a slightly different layout. It also incorporates both functions of finding devices and friends. Figure 15-3 is your Find My for macOS guide.

Most options don't need explanation, some were explained in the preceding section, and the following require a little more detail:

- **People and Devices tabs:** Click the People tab to find your friends, and click the Devices tab to find your Apple devices.
- **Device menu:** Click a device in the Devices list to find it on the map, and then click the information icon (circled *i*) to open the Device menu. From there you can play a sound, mark it as lost to lock it, or erase it.
- **Share My Location (not shown in Figure 15-3):** Click the People tab, and then click the Share My Location button in the lower left to share your location with others. When the Share My Location window opens, add the names, phone numbers, or email addresses of the people with whom you want to share your location, and then click the Send button in the upper right.

iOS and iPadOS

Find My for iOS and iPadOS are nearly identical, and both incorporate the functions of finding devices and people from the same app. Figure 15-4 shows the way around Find My for your iPhone and iPad.

Again, most of the options don't need explanation, but let's look at a couple that do:

- **Functions icons:** Tap People to find your friends, tap Devices to find your Apple devices, and tap Me to share your location.

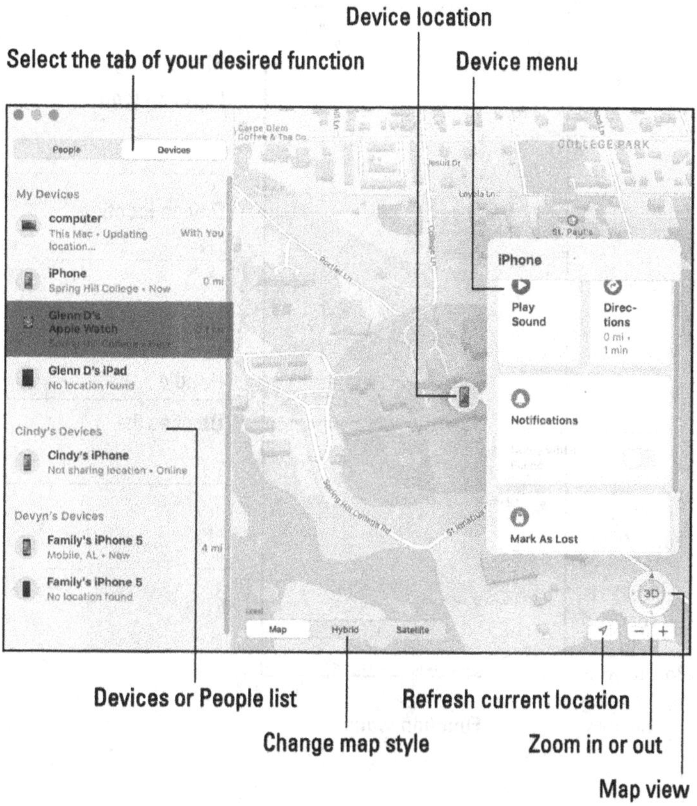
Device location
Select the tab of your desired function
Device menu
People
Devices
My Devices
computer
iPhone
Glenn D's iPad
No location found
Cindy's Devices
Cindy's iPhone
Devyn's Devices
Family's iPhone 5
Family's iPhone 5
iPhone
Play Sound
Directions
Notifications
Mark As Lost
Map
Hybrid
Satellite
3D
Devices or People list
Refresh current location
Change map style
Zoom in or out
Map view

FIGURE 15-3: Find devices and friends from your Mac.

- **Devices list:** Tap a device in the Devices list to find it on the map and open its Device menu, where you can play a sound, mark it as lost to lock it, or erase it.
- **Handle:** Drag the handle up or down to expand or collapse a menu.
- **Location icon:** Tap the Location button once to refresh your current location. Tap it twice to use the compass function for even more guidance in finding your device.

For more information regarding Find My, please check out Apple's Find My Support site at `https://support.apple.com/find-my`.

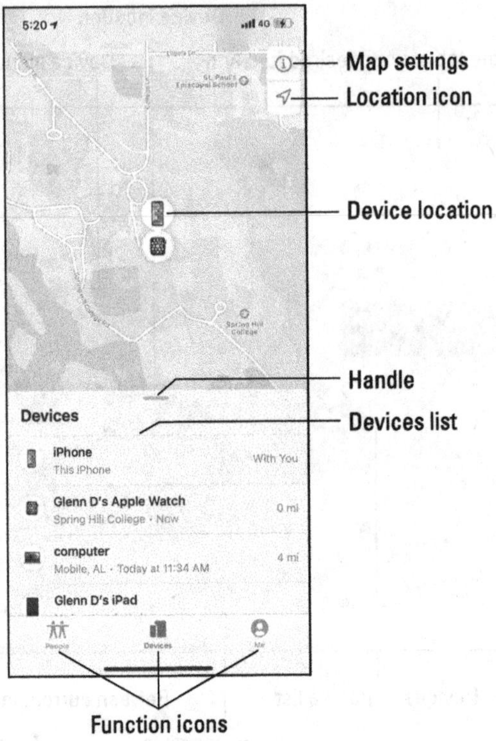
Map settings
Location icon
Device location
Handle
Devices list
Function icons
5:20
Devices
iPhone
This iPhone
With You
Glenn D's Apple Watch
Spring Hill College · Now
0 mi
computer
Mobile, AL · Today at 11:34 AM
4 mi
Glenn D's iPad
People
Devices
Me

FIGURE 15-4: Find My for iOS and iPadOS is ready to help you locate your missing devices.

5 The Part of Tens

IN THIS PART . . .

Discovering third-party apps to use with Apple Services

Exploring tips and tricks for Apple Services

IN THIS CHAPTER

» Finding new ways to use Apple services

» Discovering apps that enhance your experiences

Chapter 16 Ten Alternative Apps

Sometimes you need a fresh perspective, a new outlook on things, to get the most out of something. Case in point: Apple's Music app is good, but let's not pretend that it's great. Apple's Mail is also a good app, but it's not what die-hard email users would deem irreplaceable. Occasionally, good just isn't good enough. That's where third-party developers come in. Let's meet a few apps created by non-Apple programmers that work as well or better with some Apple services than the apps they're intended for.

MARVIS PRO

Marvis Pro is one of the top Apple Music alternatives. The app takes a minimalist approach in its user interface but allows full access to your music library. Marvis Pro is only for iOS or iPadOS and can be found in the App Store. You must have the Apple Music app installed on your iPhone or iPad for Marvis Pro to work correctly.

SOOR

Soor is one of the first music apps to integrate access to your Apple Music subscription, and therefore is among the most popular Apple Music app alternatives. Soor can be found in the iOS and iPadOS App Stores but isn't available for other platforms.

SPARK

Spark is an email client that claims to make you "love your email again" (their words), and based on tons of reviews, they're able to back up the talk. Spark has apps for macOS, iOS, iPadOS, and Android, so switching from device to device won't cause too much confusion.

MICROSOFT OUTLOOK

Outlook used to be a bloated joke on Apple devices, but no longer. Honestly, Outlook is a great email and calendar app that offers apps for macOS, iOS, iPadOS, Windows, and Android. (Find it in the App Store for your device.) It's hard to beat for the number of compatible systems alone, but it also offers a truly powerful set of features.

AIRMAIL

Airmail is an email app that works on macOS, iOS, and iPadOS. Simply look for it on your Mac, iPhone, or iPad App Store. Airmail's claim to fame is the long list of services it integrates with, including iCloud (of course). Get it in your device's App Store.

FANTASTICAL

When it comes to third-party calendar apps, Fantastical has become one of the darlings in the Apple world. It consistently garners rave reviews and even won the Mac App Store's App of the Year award for 2020. This is an Apple-only product: It works with macOS, iOS, iPadOS, and watchOS but not Windows or Android.

BUSYCAL

BusyCal is a powerful Calendar replacement that syncs with Reminders, iCloud, Exchange, Google, and other calendar and task management platforms. Its Info Panel feature helps you easily view and edit events with little to no fuss. Find it in the macOS, iOS, and iPadOS App Stores.

BUSYCONTACTS

BusyContacts is a popular contact manager that utilizes tags to help sort, categorize, and filter your contacts easily. It's a great app, but be aware that it currently supports only macOS, where it can be downloaded from the App Store.

CARDHOP

Cardhop is a premium contact manager that utilizes a natural-language search function to separate it from the pack. It was created by Flexibits, who also make the aforementioned Fantastical, and is a Mac App Store Editor's Choice. Find it in the App Store for macOS, iOS, and iPadOS.

GOODTASK

Reminders and Calendar are good, but GoodTask makes them better. GoodTask is a task manager that syncs perfectly with iCloud, so tasks you create in GoodTask sync with Reminders and Calendar, and vice versa. GoodTask's customization and organization features take it a step above the default Apple apps. It works with macOS, iOS, and iPadOS, and can be found on their respective App Stores.

IN THIS CHAPTER

» Discovering alternate ways to access Apple One services

» Enhancing your Apple One experiences

Chapter 17 Ten Tips and Tricks

I tried to cover as many bases as possible, but there's still more you can do to get the most out of your Apple One services. This chapter shares a few ideas and suggestions so you can squeeze a bit more juice out of this apple (or Apple).

REBOOT YOUR APPLE TV REMOTELY

If things go a little wonky with your Apple TV, it's a good idea to simply reboot it. To do so without having to unplug it and plug it back, reboot it using your Apple TV's remote control. Simply press and hold down on the Home and Menu buttons simultaneously until the status light on the box begins to blink, and then let go — your Apple TV reboots.

GARAGEBAND SYNC VIA ICLOUD

GarageBand is an Apple app that lets you create your own tunes, and it works on macOS, iOS, and iPadOS. If you'd like to access the same projects on all your devices, simply sync them with iCloud. Go to Apple's Support site at `https://support.apple.com`, type *use iCloud with GarageBand for* in the Search Support field, and press Return or Enter.

USE THIRD-PARTY PHOTO EDITORS

The Photos apps for macOS, iOS, and iPadOS are great for basic editing, but third-party apps in their respective App Stores go way beyond the Photo app's capabilities. Most access and edit the pictures in your camera roll, which automatically updates the images you sync in iCloud. Search the App Store on your device for *photo editor* and you'll find something to your liking.

LIMIT SCREEN TIME

We can all have too much of a good thing from time to time, especially when it comes to games on our devices. To help curb your appetite, Apple offers Screen Time, which allows you to set daily time limits for apps, including individual games or total gaming time. Go to `https://support.apple.com`, type *use Screen Time on* in the Search Support field, and then press Return or Enter.

HEADPHONES FOR MUSIC

Get the best pair of Bluetooth headphones or earbuds you can afford to enrich your experience with the Music app. They don't have to be expensive, either; you'd be shocked at how good some of the less costly brands are. Do your research to find what suits you.

DOWNLOAD MAGAZINES IN APPLE NEWS

A good Internet connection isn't always guaranteed, so if you'd like to download a magazine and read it at your leisure, go to Apple News. Of course, you'll need an Apple News+ subscription to do so. Find out more at `https://support.apple.com/en-us/HT209548`.

FREE UP SOME SPACE

Downloading media content to your device uses up valuable storage space and eventually takes a toll. Deleting movies, TV shows, music and music videos, and other media files will give your device much-needed breathing room. Go to `https://support.apple.com/en-us/HT204343` to find out how to free up space on your Mac, iPhone, iPad, and even Android devices. Your device will thank you by allowing you to download other stuff and by simply operating more smoothly. A happy device equates to a happy user.

GAME CENTER

Game Center lets you invite friends to play games across your Apple devices. Create an account using your Apple ID, and you can compete with them and other players in the Apple-verse. Check out https://support.apple.com/en-us/HT210401 for more.

ICLOUD EMAIL ALIAS

To avoid excessive spam email, create an alias for your iCloud email account. Refer to https://support.apple.com/guide/icloud/use-email-aliases-mm6b1a490a/icloud for much more on using iCloud aliases.

PIN A NOTE

Pin notes in the Notes app to keep them handy at the top of your list. To pin a note on macOS, right-click or Control-click the note and select Pin Note. For iOS and iPadOS, simply swipe right on the note in the list and tap the Pin button.

Index

A

accessing
- Apple Arcade, 54–56
- Apple Calendar, 134–136
- Apple Fitness+ (app), 74–75
- Apple Music, 36–39
- Apple News+ (app), 64–66
- Apple TV+ (app), 46–49
- Contacts (app), 161
- iCloud, 84, 90–91
- iCloud Drive, 94–99
- iCloud Mail (app), 121–123
- iCloud Photos, 108–110
- iWork apps, 168–170
- movies, 51
- music, 41
- Notes (app), 154–155
- Reminders (app), 142–144

Airmail (app), 196

AirPlay, 42

alias in iCloud Mail (app), 201

Android device
- Apple Music on, 38–43
- overview, 29

animations in slides, 184

App Store, 54

Apple Arcade
- on Apple TV, 55–56, 59
- on iPad, 54–55, 57–58
- on iPhone, 54–55, 57–58
- on Mac, 55, 58
- overview, 13–14, 53

Apple Books, 175

Apple Calendar
- accessing, 134–136
- calendars in, 137–140
- creating events, 140–141
- navigating, 136–137
- Outlook and, 135–136
- overview, 16, 84–85
- third-party apps and, 136
- website, 136

Apple Fitness+ (app)
- on Apple TV, 75
- on iPad, 74–75
- on iPhone, 74–75
- navigating, 75–79
- overview, 15–16, 73
- workouts on, 76–79

Apple Music
- on Android, 38–43
- on browsers, 39, 43–44
- on iPad, 36–37, 40–43
- on iPhone, 36–37, 40–43
- on Mac, 37, 43–44
- overview, 11–12, 35
- website for, 30
- on Windows, 37–38, 43–44

Apple News+ (app)
- downloading magazines in, 200
- on iPad, 64–65, 70–72
- on iPhone, 64–65, 66–70
- on Mac, 65–66, 70–72
- overview, 14–15, 63–64

Apple One
- Apple Arcade, 13–14
- Apple Fitness+, 15–16
- Apple Music, 11–12
- Apple News+, 14–15
- Apple TV+, 12–13
- browsers and, 30–31
- devices for, 19–20
- iCloud, 16–17
- overview, 10–11
- plans and pricing, 18

Apple TV (device)
Apple Arcade on, 55–56, 59
Apple Fitness+ on, 75
overview, 25–26
rebooting, 199
TV+ app on, 47–48
website for, 30
Apple TV+ (app)
Apple TV, 47–48
on devices, 49, 52
gaming consoles and, 48–49
on iPad, 46–47, 50–51
on iPhone, 46–47, 50–51
on Mac, 47, 51
overview, 12–13, 45
on platforms, navigating, 52
on smart TV, accessing, 48–49
website, accessing, 49
Apple Watch
Fitness+ and, 16
overview, 26–27
apps
Airmail, 196
Apple Calendar and third-party, 136
BusyCal, 197
BusyContacts, 197
Cardhop, 197
Fantastical, 196
GoodTask, 197
iCloud Mail (app) and third-party, 122
Marvis Pro, 195
Microsoft Outlook, 196
Reminders (app) and third-party, 143–144
Soor, 196
Spark, 196
Arcade (app)
on Apple TV, 55–56, 59
on iPad, 54–55, 57–58
on iPhone, 54–55, 57–58
on Mac, 55, 58
overview, 13–14, 53
articles
listening to, 69
reading, 68
attachments, in Notes (app), 157

B

backing up, devices, 20
Books, 175
browsers. *See* web browser
BusyCal (app), 197
BusyContacts (app), 197

C

Calendar
accessing, 134–136
calendars in, 137–140
creating events, 140–141
navigating, 136–137
Outlook and, 135–136
overview, 16, 84–85
third-party apps and, 136
website, 136
Cardhop (app), 197
casting music, 42
cellular data
Apple Arcade and, 55
Apple Music and, 36–37
Apple TV+ and, 46–47
cloud computing, 84
comma-separated values (.csv), 170–171
Contacts (app)
accessing, 161–162
navigating, 162–166
overview, 17, 85
cost of Apple One, 18
creating email address, 118–120

D

deleting emails, 128–129
devices. *See also* Android; Apple TV (device); Apple Watch; iPads; iPhones; Macs; Windows

accessing Apple Fitness+ (app) on, 74
for Apple One, 19–20
backing up, 20
gaming consoles, 48–49
gaming controllers, 55
headphones, 200
list of in Find My app, 191
locking, 188–189
syncing songs across, 36
documents. *See* files
downloading
in Apple News+ (app), 200
automatic, 54
with cellular data
Apple Arcade, 55
Apple Music, 36–37
Apple TV+ (app), 46–47
files, 174
photos, 111

E

emails
creating, 123–124
deleting, 128–129
folders for, 129–132
formatting, 124–126
marking, 128–129
organizing, 128–132
receiving, 127–128
replying, 127–128
rules for, 129–132
sending, 123–124
events (Apple Calendar), 140–141
Excel files (.xlsx), 170–171

F

Face ID, 121
family plan (iCloud), 86
Fantastical (app), 196
files
accessing in cloud, 84
browsing versions of, 175
collaborating on, 174
copying, 103–104
creating, 173
deleting, 104–105, 173
downloading, 174
in Keynote, 180–184
moving, 104
in Numbers, 176–179
in Pages, 172–175
printing, 174
protecting, 175
saving in iWork apps, 171
sharing, 174
supported formats, 102
uploading, 173
Files (app), 94–95
Find My (app)
accessing, 186–187
list of devices in, 191
navigating, 187–192
overview, 17, 85, 185
Fitness app
on Apple TV, 75
on iPad, 74–75
on iPhone, 74–75
navigating, 75–79
overview, 15–16, 73
workouts on, 76–79
folders
copying, 103–104
creating, 100–102, 173
deleting, 104–105
for emails, 129–132
managing, 102–106
moving, 104
formatting emails, 124–126
forwarding emails, 127

G

Game Center, 201
gaming consoles, 48–49
gaming controllers, 55
GarageBand, 199
GoodTask (app), 197

H

headphones, 200
health settings, syncing, 74–75

I

iCloud
  accessing, 90–91
  overview, 16–17, 84–86
  signing in to, 87–89
  storage space in, 86–87, 200–201
  support website for, 29
  syncing GarageBand via, 199
  website for, 30
iCloud Drive
  on browser
    accessing, 98–99
    creating folders in, 102
    managing folders and files in, 105–106
  files in, 102–106
  folders in, 100–106
  on iPad
    accessing, 94–95
    creating folders in, 100
    managing folders and files in, 102–104
  on iPhone
    accessing, 94–95
    creating folders in, 100
    managing folders and files in, 102–104
  on Mac
    accessing, 95–97
    creating folders in, 100–101
    managing folders and files in, 104–105
  overview, 16, 84
  on Windows
    accessing, 97–98
    creating folders in, 101
    managing folders and files in, 104–105
iCloud Mail (app)
  accessing, 120–121
  alias in, 201
  creating email address, 118–120
  emails
    creating, 123–124
    deleting, 128–129
    folders for, 129–132
    formatting, 124–126
    marking, 128–129
    organizing, 128–132
    receiving, 127–128
    replying, 127–128
    rules for, 129–132
    sending, 123–124
  Outlook and, 121–122
  overview, 16, 84, 117
  setting up account, 118–123
  third-party apps and, 122
iCloud Photos
  enabling, 108–110
  on iPad, 114–115
  on iPhone, 111–113
  on Mac, 114–115
  overview, 16, 84
  photo editors vs., 200
  website, 108, 110–111
  Windows, 109–110, 115
iCloud User Guide, 111, 132
inbox, 127
individual plan (iCloud), 86
iOS, 21–22
iPad Users Guide, 115
iPadOS, 23
iPads
  Apple Arcade on, 54–55, 57–58
  Apple Fitness+ on, 74–75

Apple Music on, 36–37, 40–43
Apple News+ on, 64–65, 70–72
Apple TV+ on, 46–47, 50–51
Contacts (app), 161–162, 165–166
Find My (app), 186–187, 190–192
iCloud Drive
accessing, 94–95
creating folders in, 100
managing folders and files in, 102–104
iCloud Mail on, 118, 120–121
iCloud Photos, 108–109, 114–115
Lost Mode, 188–189
Notes (app), 154–155
overview, 22–23
Reminders (app)
completing/deleting reminders, 150–151
lists, 145–147
syncing, 142–143
scanning documents with, 160–161
signing in to iCloud on, 89
iPhone User Guide, 113
iPhones
Apple Arcade on, 54–55, 57–58
Apple Fitness+ on, 74–75
Apple Music on, 36–37, 40–43
Apple News+ on, 64–65, 66–70
Apple TV+ on, 46–47, 50–51
Contacts (app), 161–162, 165–166
Find My (app), 186–187, 190–192
iCloud Drive
accessing, 94–95
creating folders in, 100
managing folders and files in, 102–104
iCloud Mail on, 118, 120–121
iCloud Photos, 108–109, 111–113
Lost Mode, 188–189
Notes (app), 154–155, 158–159
overview, 20–22
Reminders (app)
completing/deleting reminders, 150–151
lists, 145–147
syncing, 142–143
scanning documents with, 160–161
signing in to iCloud on, 89
iTunes, 29
iWork apps
accessing, 168–170
Keynote
overview, 17, 85, 179–184
supported file types, 171
Numbers
documents in, 176–179
overview, 17, 85, 175–179
supported file types, 170–171
overview, 168–170
Pages
documents in, 172–175
inserting page elements, 173
overview, 17, 85, 172–175
supported file types, 170
saving files in, 171

K

Keynote
documents in, 180–184
overview, 17, 85, 179–184
supported file types for, 171
Keynote Live, 183
Keynote User Guide for iCloud, 182–183

L

lists (Reminders), 145–147
lyrics, viewing, 42

M

macOS, 24–25
macOS User Guide, 115

Macs
Apple Arcade on, 55, 58
Apple Music on, 37, 43–44
Apple News+ on, 65–66, 70–72
Apple TV+ on, 47, 51
Contacts app on, 161–162, 164–165
Find My app on, 186–187, 190
iCloud Drive
accessing, 95–97
creating folders in, 100–101
managing folders and files in, 104–105
iCloud Mail on, 118–121
iCloud Photos, 108–109, 114–115
Notes (app), 154–155, 157–158
overview, 23–25
Reminders (app)
completing/deleting reminders, 150–151
lists, 145–147
syncing, 143
signing in to iCloud on, 87–88
managing folders in iCloud Drive, 102–106
marking emails, 128–129
Marvis Pro (app), 195
metadata, 114
Microsoft Outlook (app), 196
movies
accessing, 51
based on preferences, 51
file formats for in Keynote, 171
searching for, 51
music
accessing, 41
based on preferences, 41
casting, 42
controlling volume of, 42
opening playback window, 41
playhead, 42–43
radio stations, 41
searching for, 41
sharing, 41–42
syncing across devices, 36
viewing lyrics, 42
Music+ (app)
on Android, 38–39, 40–43
on browsers, 39, 43–44
on iPad, 36–37, 40–43
on iPhone, 36–37, 40–43
on Mac, 37, 43–44
overview, 11–12, 35
website for, 30
on Windows, 37–38, 43–44

N

navigating
Apple Arcade, 57–59
Apple Calendar, 136–137
Apple Fitness+ (app), 75–79
Apple Music, 40–44
Apple News+ (app)
iPad, 70–72
iPhone, 66–70
Mac, 70–72
Apple TV+ (app), 50–52
Contacts (app), 163–166
iCloud Photos, 110–115
Notes (app), 156–159
slides, 182
news
based on preferences, 67
following articles, 67, 70
listening to, 67, 69
News+ (app)
downloading magazines in, 200
on iPad, 64–65, 70–72
on iPhone, 64–65, 66–70
on Mac, 65–66, 70–72
overview, 14–15, 63–64
notes
drawing in, 159
pinning, 201

Notes (app)
accessing, 154–155
navigating
iPad, 158–159
iPhone, 158–159
Mac, 157–158
website, 156
overview, 16, 85
pinning notes in, 201
scanning documents with, 159–161
Numbers
documents in, 176–179
overview, 17, 85, 175–179
supported file types for, 170–171
Numbers User Guide for iCloud, 178

O

operating systems (OS), 20
organizing emails, 128–132
OS (operating systems), 20
Outlook
Apple Calendar and, 135–136
iCloud Mail (app) and, 121–122
Reminders (app) and, 142

P

Pages
documents in, 172–175
inserting page elements, 173
overview, 17, 85, 172–175
supported file types for, 170
Pages User Guide for iCloud, 174
passwords
in Notes (app), 157
setting for files, 175
photo editors, iCloud Photos vs., 200
photos
downloading, 111
editing, 113, 115
metadata of, 114
in Notes (app), 159
selecting, 112
sharing, 110, 113
viewing, 110, 112
Plain Text files (.txt), 170
playhead, 42–43
PowerPoint files (.pptx), 171
premier plan (iCloud), 86
presentations, 180–182
printing files, 174

R

radio stations, 41
reading articles, 68
rebooting Apple TV, 199
receiving emails, 127–128
Reminders (app)
accessing, 142–144
lists, 145–147
overview, 16, 85, 144
reminders in, 147–152
third-party apps and, 143–144
website, 144
replying emails, 127–128
resolution for videos, 46
Rich Text Format (.rtf), 170
rules for emails, 129–132

S

Screen Time, 200
sending emails, 123–124
sharing
calendars, 138–140
contacts, 165
files, 174
location, 190
news articles, 68
notes, 156–157
photos, 110, 113

signing in, to iCloud, 87–89
slides
  animations in, 184
  navigating, 182
smart TV, Apple TV+ on, 48–49
Soor (app), 196
Spark (app), 196
spreadsheets, 176
storage space
  freeing up, 200–201
  in iCloud, 86–87
syncing
  GarageBand via iCloud, 199
  health settings, 74–75
  music across devices, 36
  reminders, 142–144

T

tab-separated values (.tsv), 171
text styles, 156
third-party apps
  Apple Calendar and, 136
  iCloud Mail (app) and, 122
  Reminders (app) and, 143–144
TV+ (app)
  Apple TV, 47–48
  on devices, 49, 52
  gaming consoles and, 48–49
  on iPad, 46–47, 50–51
  on iPhone, 46–47, 50–51
  on Mac, 47, 51
  overview, 12–13, 45
  on platforms, 52
  on smart TV, 48–49
  website, 49
tvOS, 25–26

V

virtual cards (vCards), 163

W

watchOS, 26
web browser
  Apple Music on, 43–44
  Apple TV+ on, 49
  Contacts (app), 163–164
  Find My (app), 186, 188–189
  iCloud Drive
    creating folders in, 102
    managing folders and files in, 105–106
    overview, 98–99
  iCloud Mail on, 122–123
  iCloud Photos, 108, 110–111
  Notes (app), 156
  Reminders (app), 144
  signing in to iCloud on, 90–91
Windows computer
  Apple Music on, 37–38, 43–44
  iCloud Drive
    creating folders in, 101
    managing folders and files in, 104–105
    overview, 97–98
  iCloud on, 85
  iCloud Photos, 109–110, 115
  overview, 28–29
  Reminders (app) and, 142
Word files (.docx), 170

About the Author

Dwight Spivey has been a technical author and editor for well over a decade, but he's been a bona fide technophile for nearly four of them. He's the author of *iPhone For Seniors For Dummies,* 10th Edition (Wiley), *iPad For Seniors For Dummies,* 12th Edition (Wiley), *Idiot's Guide to Apple Watch* (Alpha), *Home Automation For Dummies* (Wiley), *How to Do Everything Pages, Keynote & Numbers* (McGraw-Hill), and many more books covering the tech gamut.

Dwight is also the educational technology administrator at Spring Hill College. His technology experience is extensive, consisting of macOS, iOS, Android, Linux, and Windows operating systems in general, educational technology, learning management systems, desktop publishing software, laser printers and drivers, color and color management, and networking.

Dwight lives on the Gulf Coast of Alabama with his wife, Cindy, their four children, Victoria, Devyn, Emi, and Reid, and their pets, Rocky, Penny, and Luna.

Dedication

To Uncle Preston and Uncle Winston, with great love and admiration. Looking forward to hearing you both sing again.

Author's Acknowledgments

Cindy, my love, thank you for keeping everything else in our lives running like clockwork so that I can do my thing. I cannot do this without you.

Carole Jelen, agent extraordinaire, you are a godsend.

Susan Pink, I cannot thank you enough. Your patience, persistence, and guidance have been amazing to behold. I've worked with lots of editors, and while they've all been great, you are top tier. Not to mention that you have one of the coolest names on the planet, just sayin'.

Much gratitude to Steve Hayes for trusting me with these projects, Ryan Williams for his technical expertise, and the other editors, designers, and professionals at Wiley who make these books such a pleasure to both read and write. Thanks so much to each and every one of you.

Publisher's Acknowledgments

Executive Editor: Steve Hayes
Project Editor: Susan Pink
Copy Editor: Susan Pink
Technical Editor: Ryan Williams
Proofreader: Debbye Butler

Production Editor: Tamilmani Varadharaj
Cover Image: © Westend61/ Getty Images

PERSONAL ENRICHMENT

Staying Sharp
dummies

9781119187790
USA $26.00
CAN $31.99
UK £19.99

Facebook
dummies

9781119179030
USA $21.99
CAN $25.99
UK £16.99

Guitar
dummies

9781119293354
USA $24.99
CAN $29.99
UK £17.99

Investing
dummies

9781119293347
USA $22.99
CAN $27.99
UK £16.99

Beekeeping
dummies

9781119310068
USA $22.99
CAN $27.99
UK £16.99

Digital Photography
dummies

9781119235606
USA $24.99
CAN $29.99
UK £17.99

Meditation
dummies

9781119251163
USA $24.99
CAN $29.99
UK £17.99

Pregnancy
dummies
6
Books

9781119235491
USA $26.99
CAN $31.99
UK £19.99

Samsung Galaxy S7
dummies

9781119279952
USA $24.99
CAN $29.99
UK £17.99

iPhone
dummies

9781119283133
USA $24.99
CAN $29.99
UK £17.99

Crocheting
dummies

9781119287117
USA $24.99
CAN $29.99
UK £16.99

Nutrition
dummies

9781119130246
USA $22.99
CAN $27.99
UK £16.99

PROFESSIONAL DEVELOPMENT

Windows 10
dummies

9781119311041
USA $24.99
CAN $29.99
UK £17.99

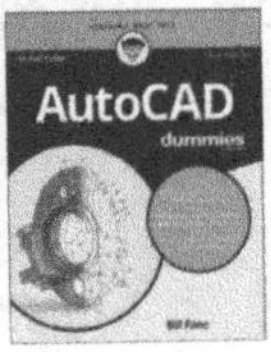
AutoCAD
dummies

9781119255796
USA $39.99
CAN $47.99
UK £27.99

Excel 2016
dummies

9781119293439
USA $26.99
CAN $31.99
UK £19.99

QuickBooks 2017
dummies

9781119281467
USA $26.99
CAN $31.99
UK £19.99

macOS Sierra
dummies

9781119280651
USA $29.99
CAN $35.99
UK £21.99

LinkedIn
dummies

9781119251132
USA $24.99
CAN $29.99
UK £17.99

Windows 10
dummies
10
Books

9781119310563
USA $34.00
CAN $41.99
UK £24.99

SharePoint 2016
dummies

9781119181705
USA $29.99
CAN $35.99
UK £21.99

Fundamental Analysis
dummies

9781119263593
USA $26.99
CAN $31.99
UK £19.99

Networking
dummies

9781119257769
USA $29.99
CAN $35.99
UK £21.99

Office 2016
dummies

9781119293477
USA $26.99
CAN $31.99
UK £19.99

Office 365
dummies

9781119265313
USA $24.99
CAN $29.99
UK £17.99

Salesforce.com
dummies

9781119239314
USA $29.99
CAN $35.99
UK £21.99

Coding
dummies

9781119293323
USA $29.99
CAN $35.99
UK £21.99

dummies.com

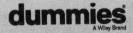

dummies
A Wiley Brand